RECURRENT NEURAL NETWORKS FOR TEMPORAL DATA PROCESSING

Edited by **Hubert Cardot** and **Romuald Boné**

Recurrent Neural Networks for Temporal Data Processing
Edited by Hubert Cardot and Romuald Boné

Published by InTech
Janeza Trdine 9, 51000 Rijeka, Croatia

Publishing Process Manager Katarina Lovrecic

Technical Editor Teodora Smiljanic

Cover Designer InTech Design Team

Additional hard copies can be obtained from orders@intechopen.com

Recurrent Neural Networks for Temporal Data Processing,
Edited by Hubert Cardot and Romuald Boné
p. cm.
ISBN 978-953-307-685-0

For EU product safety concerns :
IN TECH d.o.o., Prolaz Marije Krucifikse Kozulić 3, 51000 Rijeka, Croatia,
info@intechopen.com or visit our website at intechopen.com.

Meet the editors

H. Cardot is a full professor at the University François Rabelais Tours in France since 2003. He received his PhD in 1993 from the University of Caen (France). He is head of the Pattern Recognition and Image Analysis group (20 researchers) of the LI research laboratory. His research focuses on pattern recognition and in particular neural networks and SVM for time series prediction. He teaches at the Engineers Polytechnic School of Tours.

Professor Romuald Boné received an engineering degree in 1994 and a PhD in computer science from the University of Tours, France, in 2000. He is currently the Director of the National Engineering School of the Loire Valley (Blois, France) and also a member of the Computer Science Laboratory at the University François Rabelais of Tours. His research interests include learning algorithms for neural networks and supervised image segmentation.

Contents

Preface

The RNNs (Recurrent Neural Networks) are a general case of artificial neural networks where the connections are not feed-forward ones only. In RNNs, connections between units form directed cycles, providing an implicit internal memory. Those RNNs are adapted to problems dealing with signals evolving through time. Their internal memory gives them the ability to naturally take time into account. Valuable approximation results have been obtained for dynamical systems.

During the last few years, several interesting neural networks developments have emerged such as spike nets and deep networks. This book will show that a lot of improvement and results are also present in the active field of RNNs.

In the first chapter, we will see that many different algorithms have been applied to prediction in time series. ARIMA, one of the models studied, combines three models (AR, MA and ARMA). It is compared to Elman-RNN with four different architectures.

The second chapter gives an overview of RNN for time series prediction. The algorithm BPTT is detailed then delayed connections are added resulting into two new algorithms: EBPTT and CBPTT. BPTT is also upgraded through boosting thus giving much better results especially on multi-step ahead prediction.

The third chapter presents the application of RNN to the diagnosis of Carpal Tunnel Syndrome. The RNN used in this study is Elman-RNN and the Levenberg-Marquardt learning algorithm is detailed.

The fourth chapter describes the use of neural networks to model the hysteresis phenomena encountered on human meridian systems. Models using extreme learning machine (ELM) with a non-recurrent neural network and a RNN are compared.

The fifth chapter shows the use of a dynamic RNN to model the dynamic control of human movement. From multiple signals (EMG and EEG), the goal is to find the mapping with the movement of the different parts of the body. Some relations found by the RNN help for a better understanding of motor organization in the human brain.

The sixth chapter proposes a paradigm of how the brain deals with active interaction with environment. It is based on Compact Internal Representation (CIR). The RNNs are used here to learn and retrieve these CIRs and also to predict the trajectories of moving obstacles.

We hope that this reading will give you or generate new ideas which could be applied or adapted to your research.

February 2011

Professors Hubert Cardot[1] and Romuald Boné[2,1]
[1]University François Rabelais Tours
[2]National Engineering School of the Loire Valley
France

1

Double Seasonal Recurrent Neural Networks for Forecasting Short Term Electricity Load Demand in Indonesia

Sony Sunaryo, Suhartono and Alfonsus J. Endharta
Department of Statistics, Institut Teknologi Sepuluh Nopember
Indonesia

1. Introduction

PT. PLN (*Perusahaan Listrik Negara*) is Government Corporation that supplies electricity needs in Indonesia. This electricity needs depend on the electronic tool used by public society, so that PLN must fit public electricity demands from time to time. PLN works by predicting electricity power which is consumed by customers hourly. The prediction made is based on prior electricity power use.

The prediction of amount of electricity power use is done to optimize electricity power used by customers, so that there will not be any electricity extinction. There are some methods that could be used for forecasting of amount of electricity power use, such as double seasonal ARIMA model and Neural Network (NN) method. Some researches that are related to short-term electricity power forecasting can be seen in Chen, Wang and Huang (1995), Kiartzis, Bakirtzis and Petridis (1995), Chong and Zak (1996), Tamimi and Egbert (2000), Husen (2001), Kalaitzakis, Stavrakakis and Anagnostakis (2002), Taylor (2003), Topalli and Erkmen (2003), Taylor, Menezes and McSharry (2006), and Ristiana (2008). Neural network methods used in those researches are Feed Forward Neural Network, which is known as AR-NN model. This model cannot get and represent moving average order effect in time series. Some prior researches in many countries in the world including in Indonesia showed that ARIMA model for the electricity consumption data tends to have MA order (see Taylor, Menezes and McSharry (2006) and Ristiana (2008)).

The aim of this research is to study further about other NN type, i.e. Elman-Recurrent Neural Network (RNN) which can explain both AR and MA order effects simultaneously for forecasting double seasonal time series, and compare the forecast accuracy with double seasonal ARIMA model. As a case study, we use data of hourly electricity load demand in Mengare, Gresik, Indonesia. The results show that the best ARIMA model for forecasting these data is ARIMA ([1,2,3,4,6,7,9,10,14,21,33],1,8)(0,1,1)24(1,1,0)168. This model is a class of double seasonal ARIMA, i.e. daily and weekly seasonal with 24 and 168 length of periods respectively. Additionally, there are 14 innovational outliers detected from this ARIMA model.

In this study, we apply 4 different architectures of RNN particularly for the inputs, i.e. the input units are similar to ARIMA model predictors, similar to ARIMA predictors plus 14 dummy outliers, the 24 multiplied lagged of the data, and the combination of 1 lagged and

the 24 multiplied lagged plus minus 1. The results show that the best network is the last ones, i.e., Elman-RNN(22,3,1). The comparison of forecast accuracy shows that Elman-RNN yields less MAPE than ARIMA model. Thus, Elman-RNN(22,3,1) gives more accurate forecast values than ARIMA model for forecasting hourly electricity load demands in Mengare, Gresik, Indonesia.
The rest of this paper is organized as follows. Section 2 briefly introduces the forecasting methods, particularly ARIMA and NN methods. Section 3 illustrates the data and the proposed methodology. Section 4 evaluates the model's performance in forecasting double seasonal data and compares the forecasting accuracy between the RNN and ARIMA models. The last section gives the conclusion and future work.

2. Forecasting methods

There are many quantitative forecasting methods based on time series approach. In this section, we will briefly explain some methods used in this research, i.e. ARIMA model and Neural Network.

2.1 ARIMA model

One of the popular time series models and mostly used is ARIMA model. This model contains three parts, namely autoregressive (AR), moving average (MA), and mix of ARMA models (Wei, 2006). Bassically, this model model shows that there is a relationship between a value in the present (Z_t) and values in the past (Z_{t-k}), added by random value. ARIMA (*p,d,q*) model is a mixture of AR(*p*) and MA(*q*), with a non-stationery data pattern and *d* differencing order. The mathematics form of ARIMA(*p,d,q*) is

$$\phi_p(B)(1-B)^d Z_t = \theta_q(B)\, a_t \tag{1}$$

where *p* is AR model order, *q* is MA model order, *d* is differencing order, and

$$\phi_p(B) = (1 - \phi_1 B - \phi_2 B^2 - \ldots - \phi_p B^p)\,,$$

$$\theta_q(B) = (1 - \theta_1 B - \theta_2 B^2 - \ldots - \theta_q B^q)\,.$$

Generalization of ARIMA model for a seasonal pattern data, which is written as ARIMA $(p,d,q)(P,D,Q)^S$, is (Wei, 2006)

$$\phi_p(B)\Phi_P(B^s)(1-B)^d(1-B^s)^D Z_t = \theta_q(B)\Theta_Q(B^s)\, a_t \tag{2}$$

where s is seasonal period, and

$$\Phi_P(B^s) = (1 - \Phi_1 B^s - \Phi_2 B^{2s} - \ldots - \Phi_P B^{Ps})\,,$$

$$\Theta_Q(B^s) = (1 - \Theta_1 B^s - \Theta_2 B^{2s} - \ldots - \Theta_Q B^{Qs})\,.$$

Short-term (half-hourly or hourly) electricity consumption data frequently follows a double seasonal pattern, including daily and weekly seasonal. ARIMA model with multiplicative double seasonal pattern as a generalization of seasonal ARIMA model, written as ARIMA$(p,d,q)(P_1,D_1,Q_1)^{S1}(P_2,D_2,Q_2)^{S2}$, has a mathematical form as

$$\phi_p(B)\Phi_{P_1}(B^{s_1})\Phi_{P_2}(B^{s_2})(1-B)^d(1-B^{s_1})^{D_1}(1-B^{s_2})^{D_2}Z_t = \theta_q(B)\Theta_{Q_1}(B^{s_1})\Theta_{Q_2}(B^{s_2})a_t \quad (3)$$

where s_1 and s_2 are periods of difference seasonal.

One of the methods that can be used to estimate the parameters of ARIMA model is Maximum Likelihood Estimation (MLE) method. The assumption needed in MLE method is that error a_t distributes normally (Box, Jenkins and Reinsel, 1994; Wei, 2006). Therefore, the cumulative distribution function is

$$f(a_t \mid \sigma_a^2) = (2\pi\sigma_a^2)^{-1/2}\exp\left(-\frac{a_t^2}{2\sigma_a^2}\right) \quad (4)$$

Because error is independent, the jointly distribution from $a_1, a_2, \ldots, a_n$ is

$$f(a_1, a_2, \ldots, a_n \mid \sigma_a^2) = (2\pi\sigma_a^2)^{-n/2}\exp\left(-\frac{1}{2\sigma_a^2}\sum_{t=1}^{n} a_t^2\right). \quad (5)$$

Error a_t can be stated as a function of Z_t, and parameters ϕ, θ, σ_a^2 and also the prior error. Generally a_t is written as

$$a_t = Z_t - \phi_1 Z_{t-1} - \ldots - \phi_p Z_{t-p} + \theta_1 a_{t-1} + \ldots + \theta_q a_{t-q}\,. \quad (6)$$

The likelihood function for parameters of ARIMA model when the observations are known is

$$L(\phi,\theta,\sigma_a^2 \mid Z) = (2\pi\sigma_a^2)^{-n/2}\exp\left(-\frac{1}{2\sigma_a^2}S(\phi,\theta)\right) \quad (7)$$

where

$$S(\phi,\theta) = \sum_{t=1}^{n}(Z_t - \phi_1 Z_{t-1} - \ldots - \phi_p Z_{t-p} + \theta_1 a_{t-1} + \ldots + \theta_q a_{t-q})^2\,. \quad (8)$$

Then, the log-likelihood function is

$$l(\phi,\theta,\sigma_a^2 \mid Z) = -\frac{n}{2}\log(2\pi) - \frac{n}{2}\log(\sigma_a^2) - \frac{1}{2\sigma_a^2}S(\phi,\theta)\,. \quad (9)$$

The maximum of the log-likelihood function is computed by finding the first-order derivative of Equation (9) to each parameter and equaling to zero, i.e.

$$\frac{\partial l(\phi,\theta,\sigma_a^2 \mid Z)}{\partial\phi} = 0\ ;\quad \frac{\partial l(\phi,\theta,\sigma_a^2 \mid Z)}{\partial\theta} = 0\ ;\quad \frac{\partial l(\phi,\theta,\sigma_a^2 \mid Z)}{\partial\sigma_a^2} = 0\,.$$

An information matrix which is notated as $I(\phi,\theta)$ is used to calculate the standard error of estimated parameter by MLE method (Box, Jenkins and Reinsel, 1994). This matrix is obtained by calculating the second-order derivative to each parameter ($\beta = (\phi, \theta)$), which is notated as I_{ij} where

$$I_{ij} = \frac{\partial^2 l(\beta, \sigma_a^2 \mid Z)}{\partial \beta_i \partial \beta_j}, \tag{10}$$

and

$$I(\beta) = -E(I_{ij}). \tag{11}$$

The variance of parameter is notated as $V(\hat{\beta})$ and the standard error is $SE(\hat{\beta})$.

$$V(\hat{\beta}) = [I(\hat{\beta})]^{-1} \tag{12}$$

and

$$SE(\hat{\beta}) = [V(\hat{\beta})]^{1/2}. \tag{13}$$

2.2 Neural Network

In general Neural Network (NN) has some components, i.e. neuron, layer, activation function, and weight. NN modeling could be seen as the network form which is including the amount of neurons in the input layer, hidden layer, and output layer, and also the activation functions. Feed-Forward Neural Network (FFNN) is the mostly used NN model for time series data forecasting (Trapletti, 2000; Suhartono, 2007). FFNN model in statistics modeling for time series forecasting can be considered as a non-linear autoregressive (AR) model. This model has a limitation, which can only represent AR effects in time series data.

One of the NN forms which is more flexible than FFNN is Recurrent Neural Network (RNN). In this model the network output is set to be the input to get the next output (Beale and Finlay, 1992). RNN model is also called Autoregressive Moving Average-Neural Network (ARMA-NN), because the inputs are not only some lags of response or target, but also lags of the difference between the target prediction and the actual value, which is known as the error lags (Trapletti, 2000). Generally, the architecture of RNN model is same with ARMA(p,q) model. The difference is RNN model employs non-linear function to process the inputs to outputs, whereas ARMA(p,q) model uses linear function. Hence, RNN model can be said as the non-linear Autoregressive Moving Average model.

There are many activation functions that could be used in RNN. In this research, tangent sigmoid function and linear function are used in hidden layer and output layer respectively. The mathematics form of tangent sigmoid function is

$$f(x) = \frac{1 - e^{-2x}}{1 + e^{-2x}}, \tag{14}$$

and linear function is $f(x) = x$. The architecture of Elman-RNN, for example ARMA(2,1)-NN and 4 neuron units in hidden layer, is shown in Fig. 1.

In general, Elman-RNN(2,4,1) or ARMA(2,1)-NN is a nonlinear model. This network has 3 inputs, such as Y_{t-1}, Y_{t-2} and residual e_{t-1}, four neuron units in the hidden layer with activation function $\Psi(\bullet)$ and one neuron in the output layer with linear function. The main

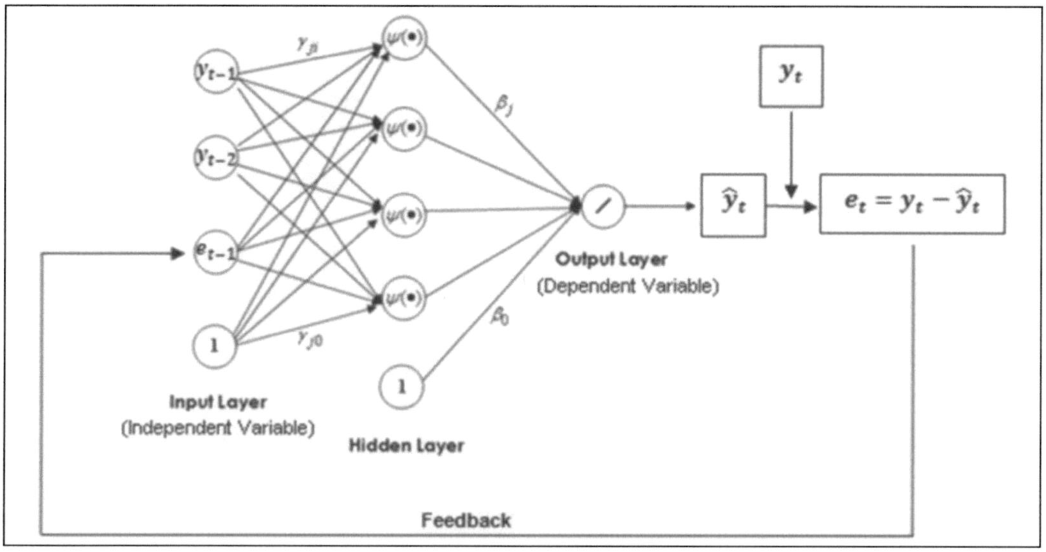

Fig. 1. The architecture of Elman-RNN(2,4,1) or ARMA(2,1)-NN

difference between Elman-RNN and other NN types is the presence of feedback process, i.e. a process representing the output as the next input. Therefore, the advantage of using Elman-RNN is the fits or predictions are usually more accurate, especially for data that consist of moving average order.

The weight and the bias in the Elman-RNN model are estimated by backpropagation algorithm. The general RNN with one hidden layer, q input units and p units in the hidden layer is

$$Y = f^{o}\left[\beta_0 + \sum_{j=1}^{p}\left(\beta_j f^{h}\left(\gamma_{j0} + \sum_{i=1}^{q}\gamma_{ji}X_i\right)\right)\right] \tag{15}$$

where β_j is the weight of the j-th unit in the hidden layer, γ_{ji} is the weight from i-th input to j-th unit in the hidden layer, $f^{h}(x)$ is the activation function in the hidden layer, and $f^{o}(x)$ is the function in the output layer. Chong and Zak (1996) explain that the weight and bias can be estimated by minimizing the value E in the following equation

$$E = \frac{1}{2}\sum_{k=1}^{n}[Y_{(k)} - \hat{Y}_{(k)}]^2 . \tag{16}$$

Minimization of Equation (16) is done by using Gradient Descent method with momentum. Gradient Descent method with momentum m, $0<m<1$, is formulated as

$$w^{(t+1)} = w^{(t)} - \left(m \cdot dw^{(t)} + (1-m)\eta\frac{\partial E}{\partial w}\right) \tag{17}$$

where dw is the change of the weight or bias, η is the learning rate which is defined, $0<\eta<1$. To solve the equation, we do the partial derivative of E to each weight and bias w with chain rules. The partial derivative of E to the weight β_j is

$$\frac{\partial E}{\partial \beta_j} = -\sum_{k=1}^{n} [Y_{(k)} - \hat{Y}_{(k)}] f^{o'}\left(\beta_0 + \sum_{l=1}^{p} \beta_l V_{l(k)} \right) V_{j(k)} \cdot \tag{18}$$

Equation (18) is simplified into

$$\frac{\partial E}{\partial \beta_j} = -\sum_{k=1}^{n} \delta^o{}_{(k)} V_{j(k)} \tag{19}$$

where

$$\delta^o{}_{(k)} = [Y_{(k)} - \hat{Y}_{(k)}] f^{o}\left(\beta_0 + \sum_{l=1}^{p} \beta_l V_{l(k)} \right).$$

By using the same way, the partial derivatives of E to β_0, γ_{li}, and γ_{l0} are done, so that

$$\frac{\partial E}{\partial \beta_0} = -\sum_{k=1}^{n} \delta^o{}_{(k)}, \tag{20}$$

$$\frac{\partial E}{\partial \gamma_{ji}} = -\sum_{k=1}^{n} \left[Y_{(k)} - \hat{Y}_{(k)} \right] f^{o'}\left(\beta_0 + \sum_{l=1}^{p} \beta_l V_{l(k)} \right) \times \beta_j f^{h'}\left(\gamma_{l0} + \textstyle\sum_{i=1}^{q} \gamma_{li} X_{i(k)} \right) X_{l(k)} \tag{21}$$

or

$$\frac{\partial E}{\partial \gamma_{ji}} = -\sum_{k=1}^{n} \delta^h{}_{(k)} X_{i(k)}, \tag{22}$$

and

$$\frac{\partial E}{\partial \gamma_{j0}} = -\sum_{k=1}^{n} \delta^h{}_{(k)}, \tag{23}$$

where

$$\delta^h{}_{(k)} = \delta^o{}_{(k)} \beta_j f^{h'}(\gamma_{l0} + \textstyle\sum_{i=1}^{q} \gamma_{li} X_{i(k)}) \cdot \tag{24}$$

These derivatives process shows that the weight and the bias can be estimated by using Gradient Descent method with momentum. The the weight and the bias updating in the output layer are

$$\beta_j^{(s+1)} = \beta_j^{(s)} - \left(m \cdot dw^{(s)} + (m-1)\eta \sum_{k=1}^{n} \delta^o{}_{(k)} V_{j(k)} \right) \tag{25}$$

and

$$\beta_0^{(s+1)} = \beta_0^{(s)} - \left(m \cdot dw^{(s)} + (m-1)\eta \sum_{k=1}^{n} \delta^o{}_{(k)} \right). \tag{26}$$

The weight and the bias updating in the hidden layer are

$$\gamma_{ji}^{(s+1)} = \gamma_{ji}^{(s)} - \left(m \cdot dw^{(s)} + (m-1)\eta \sum_{k=1}^{n} \delta^{h}{}_{(k)} X_{i(k)} \right) \tag{27}$$

and

$$\gamma_{j0}^{(s+1)} = \gamma_{j0}^{(s)} - \left(m \cdot dw^{(s)} + (m-1)\eta \sum_{k=1}^{n} \delta^{h}{}_{(k)} \right). \tag{28}$$

In Equation (25) to (28), dw is the change of the related weight or bias, m is the momentum, and η is the learning rate.

3. Data and methodology

This research uses an electricity consumption data from Electrics Goverment Company (PLN) in Gresik region as a case study. The data is hourly electricity consumption data in Mengare Gresik, which is recorded from 1 August to 23 September 2007. Then, data are divided into two parts, namely in-sample for observations in period of 1 August to 15 September 2007 and out-sample dataset for 16-23 September 2007. Fig. 2 shows the time series plot of the data.

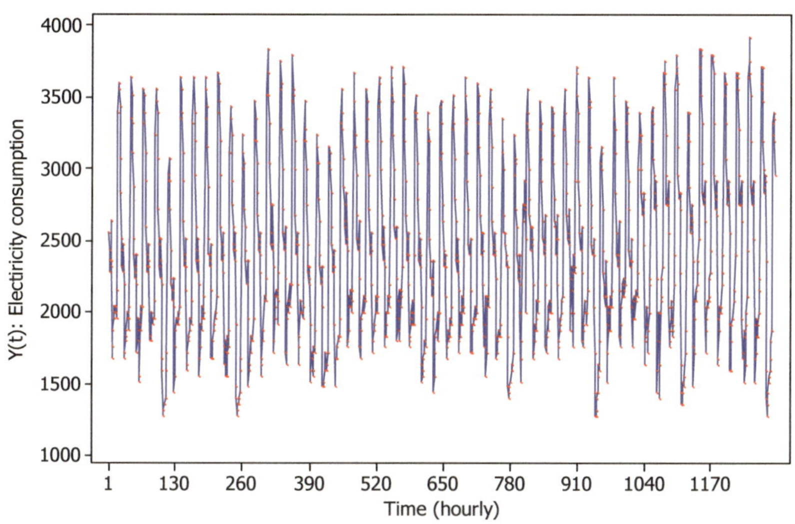

Fig. 2. Time series plot of hourly electricity consumption in Mengare Gresik, Indonesia

The methodology for analysing the data consists of the following steps:

i. Modeling of double seasonal ARIMA by using Box-Jenkins procedure.
ii. Modeling of Elman-RNN with four types of input, i.e.
    a. The inputs are based on the order of the best double seasonal ARIMA model at the first step.
    b. The inputs are based on on the order of the best double seasonal ARIMA model at the first step and dummy variables from outliers detection.
    c. The inputs are the multiplication of 24 lag up to lag 480.
    d. The inputs are lag 1 and multiplication of 24 lag ± 1.

iii. Forecast the out-sample dataset by using both Elman-RNN and double seasonal ARIMA model.
iv. Compare the forecast accuracy between Elman-RNN and double seasonal ARIMA model to find the best forecasting model.

4. Results

A descriptive data analysis shows that the highest electricity consumption is at 19.00 pm about 3537 kW, and the lowest is at 07.00 am about 1665,2 kW. This consumption explains that at 07.00 am most of customers turn the lamps off, get ready for work, and leave for the office. In Indonesia, customer work hours usually begins at 09.00 am and end at 17.00 pm. Thus, the household electricity consumption at that time period is less or beyond of the average of overall electricity consumption. At 18.00 pm, customers turn the night lamps on and at 19.00 pm most of customers have been back from work, and do many kinds of activities at house, that use a large amount of electricity such as electronics use.
Summary of descriptive statistics of the daily electricity consumption can be seen in Table 1. This table illustrates that on Tuesday the electricity consumption is the largest, about 2469.6 kW, and the lowest electricity consumption is on Sunday, about 2204.8 kW. The electricity consumption averages on Saturday and Sunday are beyond the overall average because those days are week-end days, so that customers tend to spend their week-end days with their family outside the house.

Day	Number of observations	Mean	Standard Deviation
Monday	168	2439.0	624.1
Tuesday	168	2469.5	608.2
Wednesday	192	2453.3	584.8
Thursday	192	2447.9	603.9
Friday	192	2427.3	645.1
Saturday	192	2362.7	632.4
Sunday	192	2204.8	660.3

Table 1. Descriptive Statistics of the Hourly Electricity Consumption in Every Day

4.1 Result of double seasonal ARIMA model

The process for building ARIMA model is based on Box-Jenkins procedure (Box, Jenkins and Reinsel, 1994), starting with identification of the model order from the stationer data. Fig. 2 shows that the data are non-stationer, especially in the daily and weekly periods.
Fig. 3 shows the ACF and PACF plots of the real data, and indicate that the data are non-stationer based on the slowly dying down weekly seasonal lags in ACF plot. Hence, daily seasonal differencing (24 lags) should be applied. After daily seasonal differencing, ACF and PACF plots for these differencing data are shown in Fig. 4. ACF plot shows that ACF at regular lags dies down very slowly, and indicates that regular order differencing is needed. Then, daily seasonal and regular order differencing data have ACF and PACF plots in Fig. 5. The ACF plot in this figure shows that lags 168 and 336 are significant and tend to die down very slowly. Therefore, it is necessary to apply weekly seasonal order differencing (168 lags).

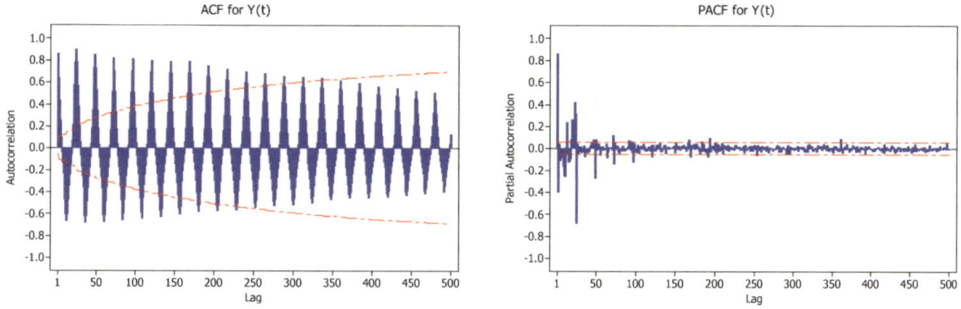

Fig. 3. ACF and PACF for original hourly electricity consumption data

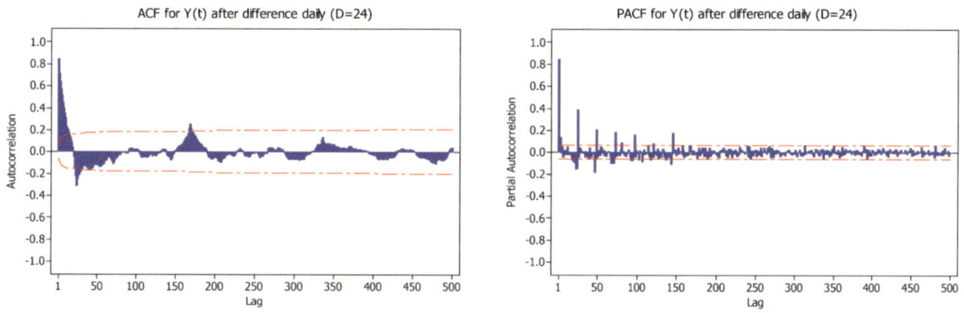

Fig. 4. ACF and PACF for data after differencing daily seasonal (D=24)

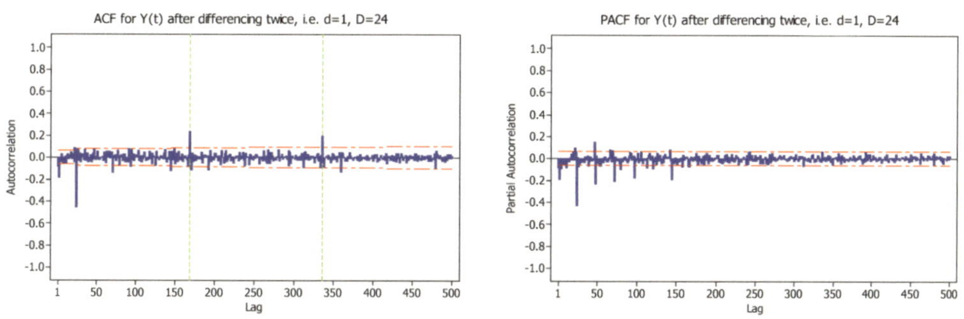

Fig. 5. ACF and PACF for data after differencing twice, i.e. d=1 and D=24

Figure 6 shows that the ACF and PACF plots of stationer data, which are the data that has been differenced by lag 1, 24, and 168. Based on these ACF and PACF plots, there are two the tentative double seasonal ARIMA models that could be proposed, i.e. ARIMA $([1,2,3,4,6,7,9,10,14,21,33],1,[8])(0,1,1)^{24}(1,1,0)^{168}$ and $([12],1,[1,2,3,4,6,7])(0,1,1)^{24}(1,1,0)^{168}$. Then, the results of parameters significance test and diagnostic check for both models show that the residuals are white noise. Moreover, the results of Normality test of the residual with Kolmogorov-Smirnov test show that the residuals for both models do not satisfy normal distribution. It due to some outliers in the data and the complete results of outliers' detection could be seen in Endharta (2009).

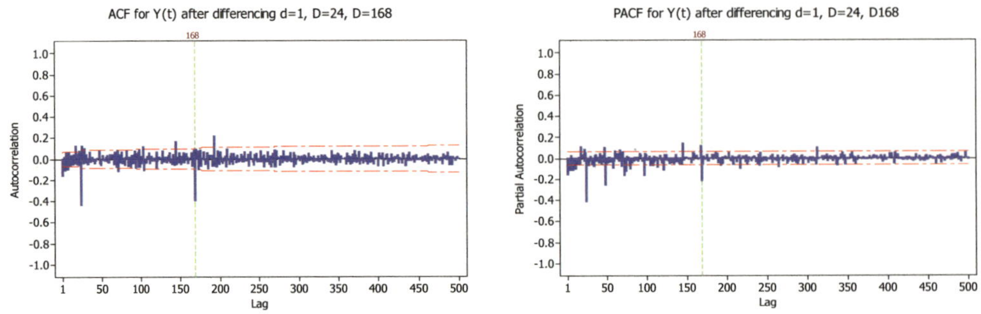

Fig. 6. ACF and PACF for stationary data after differencing d=1, D=24, and D=168.

Then, outlier detection process is only done in the first model, because MSE of this model at in-sample dataset is less than the second model. This process is done iteratively and we find 14 innovational outliers. The first model has out-sample MAPE about 22.8% and the model could be written as

$$(1+0.164B+0.139B^2+0.155B^3+0.088B^4+0.112B^6+0.152B^7+0.077B^9+0.067B^{10}+$$
$$0.069B^{14}+0.089B^{21}+0.072B^{22})(1+0.543B^{168})\,(1-B)(1-B^{24})(1-B^{168})Y_t=$$
$$(1-0.0674B^8)\,(1-0.803B^{24})a_t\,.$$

Thus, the first model with the outliers is

$$Y_t=\frac{1}{\hat{\pi}(B)}[844I_t^{(830)}-710.886I_t^{(1062)}+621.307I_t^{(906)}+-511.067I_t^{(810)}-485.238I_t^{(1027)}$$
$$-456.19I_t^{(1038)}+455.09I_t^{(274)}-438.882I_t^{(247)}+376.704I_t^{(1075)}-375.48I_t^{(971)}+$$
$$362.052I_t^{(594)}-355.701I_t^{(907)}-329.702I_t^{(623)}+308.13I_t^{(931)}+a_t]\,,$$

where

$$\hat{\pi}(B)=[(1+0.164B+0.139B^2+0.155B^3+0.088B^4+0.112B^6+0.152B^7+$$
$$0.077B^9+0.067B^{10}+0.069B^{14}+0.089B^{21}+0.072B^{22})(1+0.543B^{168})$$
$$(1-B)(1-B^{24})(1-B^{168})]/[(1-0.0674B^8)\,(1-0.803B^{24})]\,.$$

4.2 Result of Elman-Recurrent Neural Network

The Elman-RNN method is applied for obtaining the best network for forecasting electricity consumption in Mengare Gresik. The network elements are the amount of inputs, the amount of hidden units, the amount of outputs, and the activation function in both hidden and output layer. In this research, the number of hidden layers is only one, the activation function in the hidden layer is tangent sigmoid function, and in the output layer is linear function.

The first architecture of Elman-RNN that used for modeling the data is a network with inputs similar to the lags of the best double seasonal ARIMA model. This network uses input lag 1, 2, 3, 4, 5, 6, 7, 8, 9, 10, 11, 14, 15, 21, 22, 24, 25, 26, 27, 28, 29, 30, 31, 32, 33, 34, 35,

38, 39, 45, 46, 57, 58, 168, 169, 170, 171, 172, 173, 174, 175, 176, 177, 178, 179, 182, 183, 189, 190, 192, 193, 194, 195, 196, 197, 198, 199, 200, 201, 202, 203, 206, 207, 213, 214, 225, 226, 336, 337, 338, 339, 340, 341, 342, 343, 344, 345, 346, 347, 350, 351, 357, 358, 360, 361, 362, 363, 364, 365, 366, 367, 368, 369, 370, 371, 374, 375, 381, 382, 393, dan 394. Moreover, the network that was constructed with these input lags is Elman-RNN(101,3,1) and yields MAPE 4.22%.

Then, the second network uses the lags of the best double seasonal ARIMA input and adds 14 detected outliers. These inputs are the lags input as the first network and 14 outliers, i.e. in time period 803th, 1062th, 906th, 810th, 1027th, 1038th, 274th, 247th, 1075th, 971th, 594th, 907th, 623th, and 931th. This network is Elman-RNN(115,3,1) and yields MAPE 4.61%. Furthermore, the third network is network with multiplication of 24 lag input, i.e. inputs are lag 24, 48, …, 480. This third network is Elman-RNN(20,6,1) and yields MAPE 7.55%. Finally, the last network is lag 1 input and multiplication of 24 lag ± 1. The inputs of this fourth network are lag 1, 23, 24, 25, 47, 48, 49, ..., 167, 168, and 169. The network with this inputs is Elman-RNN(22,3,1) and yields MAPE 2.78%.

The forecast accuracy comparison between Elman-RNN models can be seen in Table 2. Based on criteria MSE and MAPE at the out-sample dataset, it can be concluded that Elman-RNN(22,3,1) is the best Elman-RNN for forecasting hourly electricity consumption in Mengare Gresik.

Network	In-Sample Criteria			Out-Sample Criteria	
	AIC	SBC	MSE	MAPE	MSE
RNN(101,3,1)	11.061	12.054	9778.1	4.2167	17937.0
RNN(115,3,1)	10.810	12.073	6755.1	4.6108	21308.0
RNN(20,6,1)	11.468	11.413	22955.0	7.5536	44939.0
RNN(22,3,1)	10.228	9.606	8710.7	2.7833	6943.2

Table 2. The values of each selection criteria of Elman-RNN models

4.3 Comparison between Double Seasonal ARIMA and Elman-RNN

The result of forecast accuracy comparison between double seasonal ARIMA model with and without outliers detection shows that the best model for hourly electricity consumption data forecasting in Mengare is ARIMA([1,2,3, 4,6,7,9,10,14,21,33],1,8)$(0,1,1)^{24}(1,1,0)^{168}$. Then, the comparison is also done with Elman-RNN models. The graphs of the comparison among forecasted values and residuals for the out-sample dataset can be seen in Figure 7. These results show that the residual of Elman-RNN is near to zero compared with ARIMA model. Moreover, the results also show that the forecasted values of Elman-RNN is more accurate than ARIMA model.

In addition, the comparison of forecast accuracy is also done for iterative out-sample MAPE and the result is shown in Fig. 8. This figure shows that Elman-RNN(22,3,1) gives less forecast errors than double seasonal ARIMA and other Elman-RNN models. Hence, all the results of the forecast accuracy comparison show that Elman-RNN yield more accurate forecasted values than double seasonal ARIMA model for electricity consumption data in Mengare Gresik

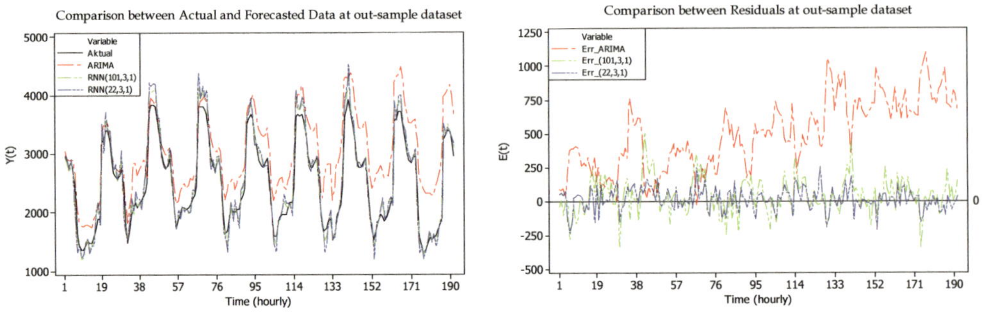

Fig. 7. The comparison of forecast accuracy between ARIMA, Elman- RNN(101,3,1), and Elman-RNN(22,3,1) model.

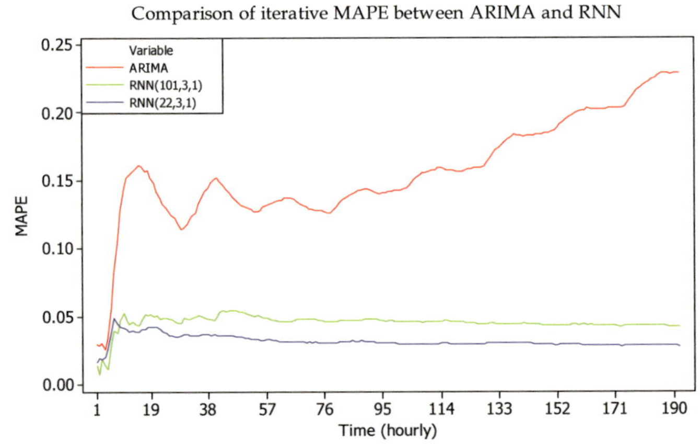

Fig. 8. The comparison of iterative MAPE at out-sample dataset.

5. Conclusion and future work

In this paper, we have discussed the application of RNN for forecasting double seasonal time series. Due to the selection of the best inputs of RNN, the identification of lags input based on double seasonal ARIMA could be used as one of candidate inputs. Moreover, the pattern of the data and the relation to the appropriate lags of the series are important information for determining the best inputs of RNN for forecasting double seasonal time series data. Short-term electricity consumption in Mengare Gresik, Indonesia has been used to compare the forecasting accuracy between RNN and ARIMA models.

The results show that the best order of ARIMA model for forecasting these data is ARIMA ([1-4,6,7,9,10,14,21,33],1,8)$(0,1,1)^{24}(1,1,0)^{168}$ with MSE 11417.426 at in-sample dataset, whereas the MAPE at out-sample dataset is 22.8%. Meanwhile, the best Elman-RNN to forecast hourly short-term electricity consumption in Mengare Gresik is Elman-RNN(22,3,1) with inputs lag 1, 23, 24, 25, 47, 48, 49, 71, 72, 73, 95, 96, 97, 119, 120, 121, 143, 144, 145, 167, 168, and 169, and activation function in the hidden layer is tangent sigmoid function and in the output layer is linear function. This RNN network yields MAPE 3% at out-sample dataset. Hence, the comparison of forecast accuracy shows that Elman-RNN method, i.e. Elman-

RNN(22,3,1), yields the most accurate forecast values for hourly electricity consumption in Mengare Gresik.

In addition, this research also shows that there is a restriction in statistics program, particularly SAS which has facility to do outlier detection. Up to now, SAS program unable to be used for estimating the parameters of double seasonal ARIMA model with adding outlier effect from the outlier detection process. This condition gives opportunity to do a further research related to the improvement of facility at statistics program, especially for double seasonal ARIMA model that involves many lags and the outlier detection.

6. References

Beale, R. & Finlay, J. (1992). *Neural Networks and Pattern Recognition in Human-Computer Interaction*. Ellis Horwood, ISBN:0-136-26995-8, Upper Saddle River, NJ, USA.

Box, G.E.P., Jenkins, G.M. & Reinsel. G.C. (1994). *Time Series Analysis Forecasting and Control, 3rd edition*. Prentice Hall, ISBN: 0-130-60774-6, New Jersey, USA.

Chen, J.F., Wang, W.M. & Huang, C.M. (1995). Analysis of an adaptive time-series autoregressive moving-average (ARMA) model for short-term load forecasting. *Electric Power Systems Research*, 34, 187-196.

Chong, E.K.P. & Zak, S.H. (1996). *An Introduction to Optimization*. John Wiley & Sons, Inc., ISBN: 0-471-08949-4, New York, USA.

Endharta, A.J. (2009). *Forecasting of Short Term Electricity Consumption by using Elman-Recurrent Neural Network*. Unpublished Final Project, Department of Statistics, Institut Teknologi Sepuluh Nopember, Indonesia.

Husen, W. (2001). *Forecasting of Maximum Short Term Electricity Usage by implementing Neural Network*. Unpublished Final Project, Department of Physics Engineering, Institut Teknologi Sepuluh Nopember, Indonesia.

Kalaitzakis, K., Stavrakakis, G.S. & Anagnostakis, E.M. (2002). Short-term load forecasting based on artificial neural networks parallel implementation. *Electric Power Systems Research*, 63, 185-196.

Kiartzis S.J., Bakirtzis, A.G. & Petridis, V. (1995). Short-term loading forecasting using neural networks. *Electric Power Systems Research*, 33, 1-6.

Ristiana, Y. 2008. *Autoregressive Neural Network Model (ARNN) for Forecasting Short Term Electricity Consumption at PT. PLN Gresik*. Unpublished Final Project, Department of Statistics, Institut Teknologi Sepuluh Nopember, Indonesia.

Suhartono. (2007). *Feedforward Neural Networks for Time Series Forecasting*. Unpublished PhD Dissertation, Department of Mathematics, Gadjah Mada University, Indonesia.

Taylor, J.W. (2003). Short-term electricity demand forecasting using double seasonal exponential smoothing. *Journal of the Operational Research Society*, 54, 799–805.

Tamimi, M. & Egbert, R. (2000). Short term electric load forecasting via fuzzy neural collaboration. *Electric Power Systems Research*, 56, 243-248.

Taylor, J.W., Menezes, L.M. & McSharry, P.E. (2006). A comparison of univariate methods for forecasting electricity demand up to a day ahead. *International Journal of Forecasting*, 22, 1-16.

Topalli, A.K. & Erkmen, I. (2003). A hybrid learning for neural networks applied to short term load forecasting. *Neurocomputing*, 51, 495-500.

Trapletti, A. (2000). *On Neural Networks as Statistical Time Series Models.* Unpublished PhD Dissertation, Institute for Statistics, Wien University.

Wei, W.W.S. (2006). *Time Series Analysis: Univariate and Multvariate Methods.* 2nd Edition, Addison Wesley, ISBN: 0-321-32216-9, Boston, USA.

2

Advanced Methods for Time Series Prediction Using Recurrent Neural Networks

Romuald Boné[1,2] and Hubert Cardot[2]
[1]National Engineering School of Loire Valley
[2]University François Rabelais Tours
France

1. Introduction

Time series prediction has important applications in various domains such as medicine, ecology, meteorology, industrial control or finance. Generally the characteristics of the phenomenon which generates the series are unknown. The information available for the prediction is limited to the past values of the series. The relations which describe the evolution should be deduced from these values, in the form of functional relation approximations between the past and the future values.
The most usually adopted approach to consider the future values $\hat{x}(t+1)$ consists in using a function f which takes as input a time window of fixed size M representing the recent history of the time series.

$$\mathbf{x}(t) = [x(t), x(t-\tau), \ldots, x(t-(M-1)\tau)] \tag{1}$$

$$\hat{x}(t+\tau) = f(\mathbf{x}(t)) \tag{2}$$

where $x(t)$, for $0 \le t \le 1$, is the time series data that can be used for building a model.
Most of the current work on single-step-ahead prediction relies on a result released in (Takens, 1981) which shows that under several assumptions (among which the absence of noise), it is possible to obtain a perfect estimate of $x(t+\tau)$ according to (2) if $M \ge 2d+1$, where d is the dimension of the stationary attractor generating the time series. In this approach, the memory of the past is preserved in the sliding time window.
In multi-step-ahead prediction, given $\{x(t), x(t-\tau), \ldots, x(t-n\tau), \ldots\}$, one is looking for a good estimate $\hat{x}(t+h\tau)$ of $x(t+h\tau)$, h being the number of steps ahead.
Given their universal approximation properties, neural networks, such as multi-layer perceptrons (MLPs) or recurrent networks (RNs), are good candidate models for the global approaches. Among the many neural network architectures employed for time series prediction, one can mention MLPs with a time window in the input (Weigend et al., 1990), MLPs with finite impulse response (FIR) connections (equivalent to time windows) both from the input to the hidden layer and from the hidden layer to the output (Wan, 1994), recurrent networks obtained by providing MLPs with a feedback from the output (Czernichow, 1996), simple recurrent networks (Suykens & Vandewalle, 1995), recurrent

networks with FIR connections (El Hihi & Bengio, 1996), (Lin et al., 1996) and recurrent networks with both internal loops and feedback from the output (Parlos et al., 2000).
But the use of these architectures for time-series prediction has inherent limitations, since the size of the time window or the number of time delays of the FIR connections is difficult to choose.
An alternative solution is to keep a small length (usually $M = 1$) time window and enable the model to develop on its own a memory of the past. This memory is expected to represent the past information that is actually needed for performing the task more accurately. Time series prediction with RNNs usually corresponds to such a solution. Memory of the past - of variable length, see e.g. (Aussem, 2002; Hammer & Tino, 2003) - is maintained in the internal state of the model, $\mathbf{s}(t)$, of finite dimension d at time t, which evolves (for $M = 1$) according to:

$$\mathbf{s}(t+\tau) = \mathbf{g}(\mathbf{s}(t), x(t)) \tag{3}$$

where $\mathbf{g}$ is a mapping function assumed to be continuous and differentiable. The time variable t can either be continuous or discrete and $\mathbf{h}$ is the output function. Assuming that the system is noise free, the observed output is related to the internal dynamics of the system by:

$$\hat{x}(t+\tau) = \mathbf{h}(\mathbf{s}(t)) \tag{4}$$

where $\hat{x}(t+\tau)$ is the estimate of $x(t+\tau)$ and the function $\mathbf{h}$ is called the measurement function.
Globally feed-forward architectures, both very common and with a short calculation time, are widely used. They share the characteristic of having been initially elaborated for using the error gradient back-propagation of feed-forward neural networks (some of which have an adapted version today (Campolucci et al., 1999)). Hence the locally recurrent globally feed-forward networks (Tsoi & Back, 1994) introduce particular neurons, with local feedback loops. In the most general form, these neurons feature delays in inputs as well as in their loops. All these architectures remain limited: hidden neurons are mutually independent and therefore, cannot pick up some complex behaviors which require the collaboration of several neurons of the hidden layer. In order to overcome this problem, a certain number of recurrent architectures have been suggested (see (Lin et al., 1996) for a presentation). It has been shown that in practice the use of delay connections in these networks gives rise to a reduction in learning time (Guignot & Gallinari, 1994) as well as an improvement in the taking into account of long term dependencies (Lin et al., 1996; Boné et al., 2002). The resulting network is named Time Delay Recurrent Neural Networks (TDRNN). In this case, unless to apply an algorithm for selective addition of connections with time delays (Boné et al., 2002), which improve forecasting performance capacity but at the cost of increasing computations, the networks finally retained are often oversized and use meta-connections with consecutive delay connections, also named Finite Impulse Response (FIR) connections or, if they contain loops, Infinite Impulse Response (IIR) connections (Tsoi & Back, 1994).
Recurrent neural networks (RNNs) is a class of neural networks where connections between neurons form a directed cycle. They possess an internal memory owing to cycles in their connection graph and do no longer need a time window to take into account the past values

of the time series. They are able to model temporal dependencies of unspecified duration between the inputs and the associated desired outputs, by using internal memory. The passage of information from one neuron to the other through a connection is not instantaneous (one time step), unlike MLP, and thus the presence of the loops makes it possible to keep the influence of the information for a variable time period, theoretically infinite. The memory is coded by the recurrent connections and the outputs of the neurons themselves. Throughout the training, the network learns how to complete three complementary tasks: the selection of useful inputs, their retention in coded form and their use in the calculation of its outputs.

RNNs are computationally more powerful than feed-forward networks (Siegelmann et al, 1997), and valuable approximation results were obtained for dynamical systems (Seidl & Lorenz, 2001).

2. RNNs learning

During the last two decades, several methods for supervised training of RNNs have been explored. BackPropagation Through Time (BPTT) is probably the most widely used method. BPTT is an adaptation of the well-known backpropagation training method known from feedforward networks. It is therefore a gradient-based training method.

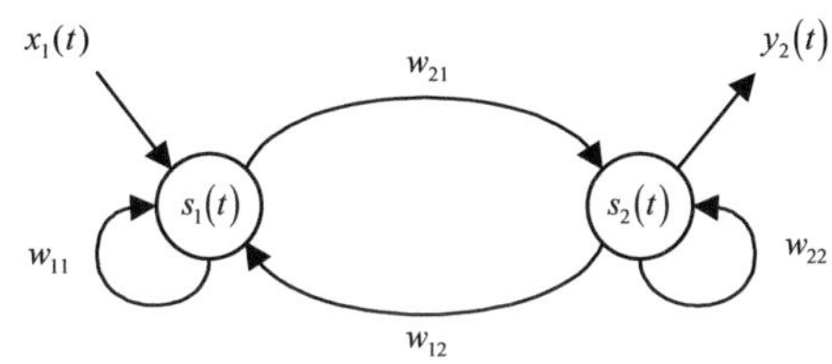

Fig. 1. A recurrent neural network

The feedforward backpropagation algorithm cannot be directly transferred to RNNs, because the backpropagation pass presupposes that the connections between the neurons induce a cycle-free ordering. Considering a time series of length l, the central idea of BPTT algorithm is to unfold the original recurrent networks (Fig. 1) in time so as to obtain a feedforward network with l layers (Fig. 2), which in turn makes it possible to apply the learning method by backpropagation of gradient of the error through time. BPTT unfolds the network in time by stacking identical copies of the RNN, and duplicating connections within the network to obtain connections between subsequent copies.

The weights between successive layers must remain identical in order to be able to show up in the original recurrent network. In practice, it amounts to cumulating the changes of the weights for all the copies of a particular connection and to adding the sum of the changes to all these copies after each learning iteration.

Let us consider the application of BPTT for the training of recurrent networks between time t_1 and t_l. f_i is the transfer function of neuron i, $s_i(t)$ its output at time t, and w_{ij} its connection from neuron j. A value, provided to the neuron at time t, coming from outside, is noted $x_i(t)$.

The algorithm supposes an evolution of neurons of recurrent networks given by the following equations:

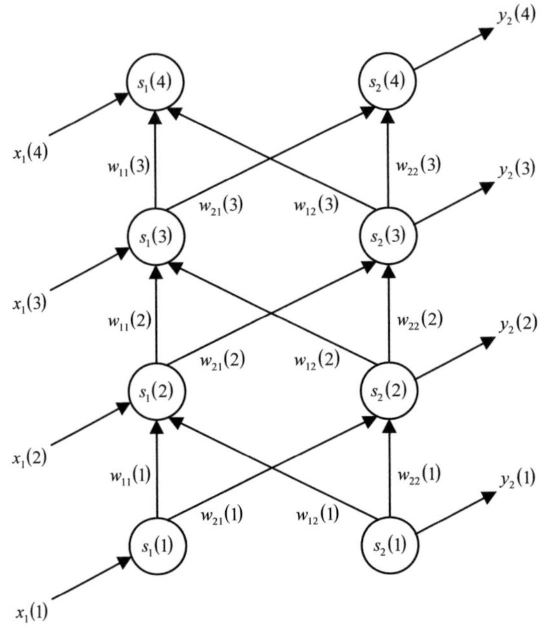

Fig. 2. RNN of Fig. 1 unfolded in time

$$s_i(t) = f(net_i(t-1)) + x_i(t)\ ;\ i = 1, \ldots, N \tag{5}$$

$$net_i(t-1) = \sum_{j \in pred(i)} w_{ij}(t-1) s_j(t-1) \tag{6}$$

The set Pred(i) contains, for each neuron i, the index of the incoming neurons $Pred(i) = \{ j \in N \mid \exists (w_{ij}, \tau_{ij}) \}$. Likewise, we have defined the successors of a neuron i: $Succ(i) = \{ j \in N \mid \exists (w_{ji}, \tau_{ji}) \}$.

The variation of the weight for all the sequence is calculated by the sum of the variations of this weight on each element of the sequence. By noting $T(\tau)$ the set of neurons which have a desired output $d_p(\tau)$ at time τ, we define the mean quadratic error $E(t_1, t_l)$ of the recurrent neural networks between time t_1 and t_l as:

$$E(t_1, t_l) = \frac{1}{2} \sum_{t=t_1}^{t_l} \sum_{p \in T(t)} (d_p(t) - s_p(t))^2 \tag{7}$$

To minimize total error, gradient descent is used to change each weight in proportion to its derivative with respect to the error, provided the non-linear activation functions are differentiable (η is the learning step):

$$\Delta w_{ij}(t_1, t_l - 1) = -\eta \frac{\partial E(t_1, t_l)}{\partial w_{ij}} = -\eta \sum_{\tau = t_1}^{t_l - 1} \frac{\partial E(t_1, t_l)}{\partial w_{ij}(\tau)} \tag{8}$$

with

$$\frac{\partial E(t_1,t_l)}{\partial w_{ij}(\tau)}=\frac{\partial E(t_1,t_l)}{\partial net_i(\tau)}\frac{\partial net_i(\tau)}{\partial w_{ij}(\tau)} \tag{9}$$

where $w_{ij}(\tau)$ is the duplication of the weight w_{ij} of the original recurrent networks, for the time $t=\tau$. We expand $\partial E(t_1,t_l)/\partial net_i(\tau)$:

$$\frac{\partial E(t_1,t_l)}{\partial net_i(\tau)}=\frac{\partial E(t_1,t_l)}{\partial s_i(\tau+1)}\frac{\partial s_i(\tau+1)}{\partial net_i(\tau)} \text{ with } \frac{\partial s_i(\tau+1)}{\partial net_i(\tau)}=f'(net_i(\tau)) \tag{10}$$

If neuron i belongs to the last layer ($\tau=t_l-1$):

$$\frac{\partial E(t_1,t_l)}{\partial s_i(\tau+1)}=\frac{\partial e(t_l)}{\partial s_i(t_l)}=\delta_{i\in T(\tau+1)}\left(s_i(t_l)-d_i(t_l)\right) \tag{11}$$

where $\delta_{i\in T(\tau+1)}=1$ if $i\in T(\tau+1)$ and 0 otherwise. If neuron i belongs to the preceding layers:

$$\frac{\partial E(t_1,t_l)}{\partial s_i(\tau+1)}=\frac{\partial e(\tau+1)}{\partial s_i(\tau+1)}+\sum_{j\in Succ(i)}\left(\frac{\partial E(t_1,t_l)}{\partial net_j(\tau+1)}\frac{\partial net_j(\tau+1)}{\partial s_i(\tau+1)}\right) \tag{12}$$

As $\partial net_j(\tau+1)/\partial s_i(\tau+1)=w_{ji}(\tau+1)$, the equations of BPTT algorithm are finally obtained:

$$\Delta w_{ij}(t_1,t_l-1)=-\eta\sum_{\tau=t_1}^{t_l-1}\frac{\partial E(t_1,t_l)}{\partial net_i(\tau)}s_j(\tau) \tag{13}$$

- with, for the output layer

$$\frac{\partial E(t_1,t_l)}{\partial net_i(\tau)}=\begin{cases}[s_i(t_l)-d_i(t_l)]f_i'(net_i(\tau)) \text{ if } i\in T(\tau+1)\\ 0 \quad \text{else}\end{cases} \tag{14}$$

- and for the hidden layer

$$\frac{\partial E(t_1,t_l)}{\partial net_i(\tau)}=\begin{cases}\left[\begin{array}{l}[s_i(\tau+1)-d_i(\tau+1)]\\ +\displaystyle\sum_{j\in Succ(i)}\frac{\partial E(t_1,t_l)}{\partial net_j(\tau+1)}w_{ji}(\tau+1)\end{array}\right].f_i'(net_i(\tau)) \text{ if } i\in T(\tau+1)\\ \displaystyle\sum_{j\in Succ(i)}\frac{\partial E(t_1,t_l)}{\partial net_j(\tau+1)}w_{ji}(\tau+1)f_i'(net_i(\tau)) \text{ else}\end{cases} \tag{15}$$

Eq. (13) to (15) allow to apply error gradient backpropagation through time: after the forward pass, witch consists in updating the unfolded network, starting from the first copy of the recurrent network and working upwards through the layers, $\partial E(t_1,t_l)/\partial net_i(\tau)$ is computed, by proceeding backwards through the layers $t_l,\ldots,t_1$.

One epoch requires O(lM) multiplications and additions, where M is the total number of network connections. Many speed-up techniques for gradient descent approach are

described in the literature, e.g. dynamic learning rate adaptation schemes. Another approach to achieve faster convergence is to use second-order gradient descent techniques.
Unfortunately, the gradient descent algorithms which are commonly used for training RNNs have several limitations, the most important one being the difficulty of dealing with long-term dependencies in the time series (Bengio et al, 1994; Hochreiter & Schmidhuber 1997) i.e. problems for which the desired output depends on the inputs presented at times far in the past.
Backpropagated error gradient information tends to "dilute" exponentially over time. This phenomenon is called "vanishing gradient" or "forgetting behavior" (Frasconi et al., 1992; Bengio et al, 1994). (Bengio et al, 1994) have demonstrated the existence of a condition on the eigenvalues of the RNN Jacobian to be able to store information for a long period of time in the presence of noise. But this implies that the portion of gradient due to information at times $\tau << t$ is insignificant compared to the portion of gradient at times near t.

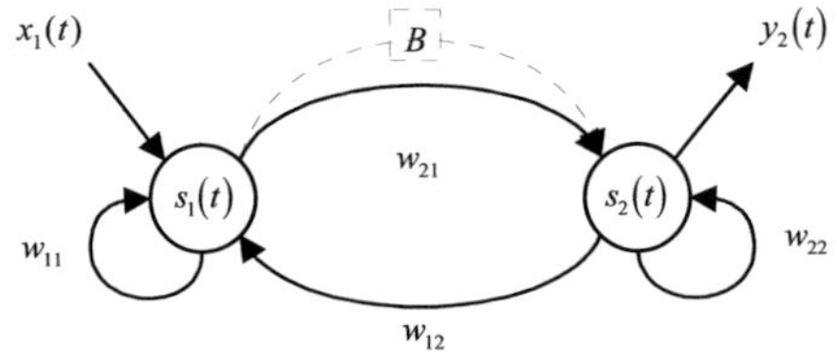

Fig. 3. Delayed connection added to a RNN (dotted line)

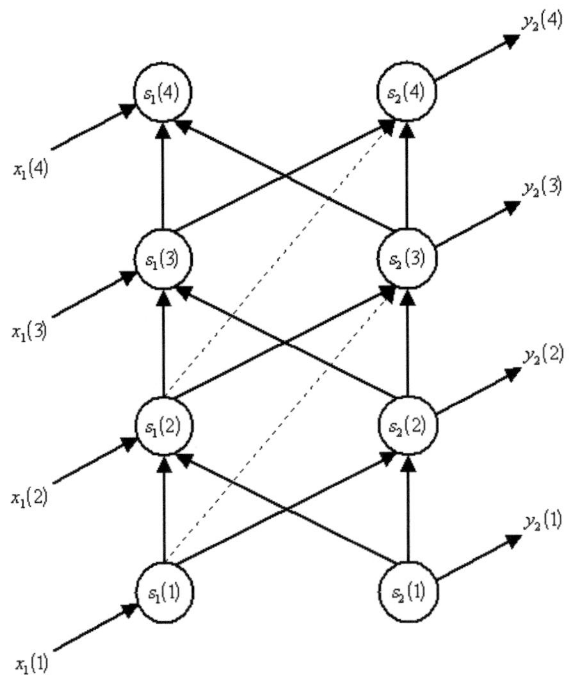

Fig. 4. The RNN of Fig. 3 unfolded in time. Duplicated dotted connections correspond to the added connection

We can give a more intuitive explanation for backpropagated gradient vanishing. Considering eq. (13) to (15), gradient calculation for each layer is done by a product with transfer function derivate. Most of the time, this last value is bounded between 0 and 1 (i.e. sigmoid function). Each time the signal is backpropagated through a layer, the gradient contribution of the forward layers is attenuated. Along the time-delayed connections the signal does no longer cross nonlinear activation functions between successive time steps (see Fig. 3 and Fig. 4).

Adding connections with time delays to the RNN (El Hihi & Bengio, 1996; Lin, T., et al., 1996) often allows gradient descent algorithms to find better solutions in these cases. Indeed, by acting as a linear link between two distant moments, such a connection has beneficial effects on the expression of the gradient. Adding a delayed connection to an RNN (Fig. 3) creates several connections in the unfolded network (Fig. 4) jumping as many layers as the delay. Gradient backpropagated by these connections avoids attenuation of intermediate layers.

But in the absence of prior knowledge concerning the problem to solve, how can one choose the locations and the delays associated to these new connections? By systematically adding meta-connections with consecutive delay connections, also named Finite Impulse Response (FIR) connections, one obtains oversized networks which are slow to train and have poor generalization abilities. Various regularization techniques can be employed in order to improve generalization and this further increases the computational cost.

Constructive approaches for adapting the architecture of a neural network are usually more economical. An algorithm for the addition of time-delayed connections to recurrent networks should start with a simple, ordinary RNN and progressively add new connections according to some heuristic. An alternative solution could be found in the learning of the connection delays themselves. We suggested, for an RNN that associates a delay to each connection, an algorithm based on the gradient which simultaneously adjusts weights and delays.

To improve the obtained results, we may also adapt general methods which authorize to improve the performances of various models. One such approach is to use a combination of models to obtain a more precise estimate than the one obtained by a single model. One such procedure is known under the name of boosting.

3. Constructive algorithms

Instead of systematically adding finite impulse response (FIR) connections to a recurrent network, each connection encompassing a whole range of delays, we opted for a constructive approach: starting with an RN having no time-delayed connections, then selectively adding a few such connections. The two algorithms we present in the following allow us to choose the location and the delay associated with a time-delayed connection which is added to an RN. The assumption we make is that significantly better results can be obtained by the addition of a small number of time-delayed connections to a recurrent network. The reader is invited to consult (Boné et al., 2000a; Boné et al, 2000b; Boné et al., 2002) for a more detailed discussion regarding the role of time-delayed connections in RNs. The iterative and constructive aspects diminish the effect of the vanishing gradient on the outcome of the algorithm. Indeed, by reinforcing the long-term dependencies in the network, the first time-delayed connections favor the subsequent learning steps. A high selectivity should allow us to avoid over-parameterized networks. For every iteration, we rank the candidate connections according to their relevance.

We retained two alternative methods for defining the relevance of a candidate connection. The first one is based on the amount by which the error diminishes after the addition of the connection. The second one relies on a more detailed study of various quantities computed inside the network during gradient descent.

3.1 Bounded exploration for the addition of time-delayed connections

The first heuristic is a breadth-first search (BFS). It explores the alternatives for the location and the delay associated with a new connection by adding that connection and performing a few iterations of the underlying learning algorithm. The connection that produces the largest increase in performance during these few iterations is then added, and the learning continues until error increases on the stop set. Another exploratory stage begins for the addition of a new connection. The algorithm eventually ends when the error on the stop set no longer decreases upon the addition of a new connection, or a (user-specified) bound on the number of new connections is reached. We employed BPTT as the underlying learning algorithm and we called this constructive algorithm Exploratory Back-Propagation Through Time (EBPTT). We must note that the breadth-first heuristic does not need any gradient information and can be applied in combination with learning algorithms which are not based on the gradient.

If the RNN we start with does not account well for the medium or long-term dependencies in the data, and these dependencies are not too complex, then by adding the appropriate connection the error is likely to diminish relatively fast.

Three new parameters are required for this constructive algorithm: the maximal value for the delay of a new connection, the maximal number of new connections and the number of BPTT steps performed for each candidate connection during the exploratory stage. In choosing the value of the first parameter one should ideally use prior knowledge related to the problem. If such information is not available one can rely on simple, linear measures such as auto or cross-correlations to find a bound for the long-term dependencies. Computational cost governs the choice of the two other parameters. However, the experiments we present in the following show that the contribution of the new connections diminishes quickly as their number increases. The complexity of the exploratory stage may seem quite high, $O(N^4)$, since after the addition of each candidate connection we carry out several steps of the BPTT algorithm on the entire network. The user is supposed to find a tradeoff between the quality of the results and the computation cost. When compared to the complete exploration of all the alternative architectures, this breadth-first search is only interesting if good results can be obtained with few learning steps during the exploratory stage. Fortunately, experimental evidence shows that this appears to be the case, so the global cost of the algorithm remains low.

3.2 Internal correlations

The second heuristic for defining the relevance of a candidate connection is closely dependent on BPTT-like underlying learning algorithms. Since this method makes use of quantities computed during gradient descent, its computation cost is significantly lower than for the breadth-first search.

When applying BPTT on the training set between t_1 and t_l, we obtain the following expression for the variation of one weight of delay k, $\Delta w_{ij}^{(k)}(t_1, t_l - 1)$:

$$\Delta w_{ij}^{(k)}(t_1, t_l - 1) = \sum_{\tau=t_1+k}^{t_l-1} \Delta w_{ij}^{(k)}(\tau) = -\eta \sum_{\tau=t_1+k}^{t_l-1} \frac{\partial E(t_1, t_l)}{\partial w_{ij}^{(k)}(\tau)} \tag{16}$$

$w_{ij}^{(k)}(\tau)$ being the copy of $w_{ij}^{(k)}$ for $t = \tau$ in the unfolded network employed by BPTT. We may write

$$\frac{\partial E(t_1, t_l)}{\partial w_{ij}^{(k)}(\tau)} = \frac{\partial E(t_1, t_l)}{\partial net_i(\tau)} \cdot s_j(\tau - k) \qquad \tau \in [t_1 + k; t_l - 1] \tag{17}$$

We are looking for connections which are potentially useful in capturing (medium or long-term) dependencies in the data. A connection $w_{ij}^{(k)}$ is then useful only if it has a significant contribution to the computation of the gradient, i.e. $\partial E(t_1, t_l)/\partial w_{ij}^{(k)}(\tau)$ is significantly different from zero for many iterations of the learning algorithm. We select the output of a neuron $s_j(\tau - k)$ which best contributes to a reduction in error by means of $\partial E(t_1, t_l)/\partial net_i(\tau)$.

The resulting algorithm, called Constructive Back Propagation Through Time (CBPTT), computes during several BPTT steps the correlation between the values of $\partial E(t_1, t_l)/\partial net_i(\tau)$ and $s_j(\tau - k)$ for $\tau \in [t_1 + k; t_l - 1]$. The relevance of a candidate connection $w_{ij}^{(k)}$ is defined as the absolute value of this correlation. The connection with the highest relevance factor is then added to the RNN, its weight is initialized to 0, and learning continues. The process stops when a new connection has no further positive effect on the performance of the RNN, as evaluated on a stop set. The time complexity and the storage complexity of CBPTT is the same as for BPTT.

This constructive algorithm requires two new parameters: the maximal value for the delays of the new connections and the maximal number of new connections. The choice of these parameters is independent from the constructive heuristic, so the rules already mentioned for EBPTT should be applied. Experiments reported in (Boné et al., 2002) support the view that the precise value of this parameter does not have a high influence on the outcome, as long as it is higher than the significant linear dependencies in the data, which are given by the autocorrelation. The same experiments show that performance is not very sensitive to the bound on the number of new connections either, because the contribution of the new connections quickly diminishes as their number increases.

This definition for the relevance of a candidate connection is well adapted to time dependencies which are well represented in the available data. If this is not the case for the dependencies one is interested in, a more thorough study of the distribution of the product $s_j(\tau - k) \cdot \partial E(t_1, t_l)/\partial net_i(\tau)$ should suggest more adequate measures for the relevance.

4. Time Delay Learning

An alternative to the adding of connections with time delays could be found in the learning of the connection delays themselves. (Duro & Santos Reyes, 1999) (see also (Pearlmutter 1990)) have suggested, for a feed-forward neural networks that associate a delay to each connection, an algorithm based on the gradient which simultaneously adjusts weights and delays. We adapted this technique to a recurrent architecture.

Considering an RNN in which two values are associated to each connection from a neuron j to a neuron i, these two values are of a usual weight w_{ij} of the signal and a delay τ_{ij} which is a real value indicating the needed time for the signal to propagate through the connection. Note that this parameter is not the same as the maximal order of a FIR connection: indeed, when we consider a connection of delay τ_{ij}, we do not have simultaneously $\tau_{ij}-1$ connections with integer delays between 1 and τ_{ij}. The neuron output $s_i(t)$ is given by:

$$s_i(t)=f_i(net_i(t-1)) \text{ with } net_i(t-1)=\sum_{j\in Pred(i)} w_{ij}s_j(t-\tau_{ij}-1) \tag{15}$$

The values $s_j(t-\tau_{ij}-1)$ are obtained by applying a linear interpolation between the two nearest whole numbers of the delay τ_{ij}.

We have adapted the BPTT algorithm to this architecture with a simultaneous learning of weights and delays of the connections, inspired from (Duro & Santos Reyes, 1999). The variation of a delay τ_{ij} can be computed as the sum of the variations of this parameter copies corresponding to the times from t_1 to t_l. Then we add this variation to all copies of τ_{ij}. We will only give here the demonstration of the learning of the delays as the learning of the weight can easily be deducted from it.

We note $\tau_{ij}(\tau)$ the copy of τ_{ij} for $t=\tau$ in the unfold in time neural net which is virtually constructed with BPTT. $\lceil . \rceil$ is the operator of upward roundness.

We apply a back-propagation of the gradient of the mean quadratic error $E(t_1,t_l)$ which is defined as the sum of the instantaneous errors $e(t)$ from t_1 to t_l:

$$E(t_1,t_l)=\sum_{t=t_1}^{t_l} e(t)=\sum_{t=t_1}^{t_l}\frac{1}{2}\sum_{p\in T(t)}(d_p(t)-s_p(t))^2 \tag{16}$$

$$\Delta\tau_{ij}(t_1,t_l-1)=-\lambda\frac{\partial E(t_1,t_l)}{\partial \tau_{ij}}=\sum_{\tau=t_1+\lceil\tau_{ij}\rceil}^{t_l-1}\Delta\tau_{ij}(\tau)=-\lambda\sum_{\tau=t_1+\lceil\tau_{ij}\rceil}^{t_l-1}\frac{\partial E(t_1,t_l)}{\partial\tau_{ij}(\tau)} \tag{17}$$

We can write $\partial E(t_1,t_l)/\partial\tau_{ij}(\tau)=\partial E(t_1,t_l)/\partial net_i(\tau)\bullet\partial net_i(\tau)/\partial\tau_{ij}(\tau)$. With a first order approximation, $\partial net_i(\tau)/\partial\tau_{ij}(\tau)\approx w_{ij}(s_j(\tau-\tau_{ij}-1)-s_j(\tau-\tau_{ij}))$. We expand $\partial E(t_1,t_l)/\partial net_i(\tau)$ following Eq. 10. If neuron i belongs to the last layer ($\tau=t_l-1$), we apply Eq. 11. If neuron i belongs to one of the preceding layers:

$$\frac{\partial E(t_1,t_l)}{\partial s_i(\tau+1)}=\frac{\partial e(\tau+1)}{\partial s_i(\tau+1)}+\sum_{j\in Succ(i)}\left(\frac{\partial E(t_1,t_l)}{\partial net_j(\tau+\tau_{ji}+1)}\frac{\partial net_j(\tau+\tau_{ji}+1)}{\partial s_i(\tau+1)}\right) \tag{18}$$

As $\partial net_j(\tau+\tau_{ji}+1)/\partial s_i(\tau+1)=w_{ji}(\tau+1)$, we obtain the final relations to learn the delay associated to each connection:

$$\Delta\tau_{ij}(t_1,t_l-1)=-\lambda\sum_{\tau=t_1+k}^{t_l-1}\frac{\partial E(t_1,t_l)}{\partial net_i(\tau)}w_{ij}(s_j(\tau-\tau_{ij}-1)-s_j(\tau-\tau_{ij})) \tag{19}$$

with for $\tau=t_l-1$

$$\frac{\partial E(t_1,t_l)}{\partial net_i(\tau)} = \underset{i \in T(\tau+1)}{\delta}(s_i(t_l) - d_i(t_l))f_i'(net_i(\tau)) \tag{20}$$

and for $t_1 \le \tau < t_l - 1$

$$\frac{\partial E(t_1,t_l)}{\partial net_i(\tau)} = \left[\begin{array}{l} \underset{i \in T(\tau+1)}{\delta}(s_i(\tau+1) - d_i(\tau+1)) \\ + \sum\limits_{j \in Succ(i)} \dfrac{\partial E(t_1,t_l)}{\partial net_j(\tau + \tau_{ji} + 1)} w_{ji}(\tau+1) \end{array} \right] f_i'(net_i(\tau)) \tag{21}$$

5. Boosting Recurrent Neural Networks

To improve the RNN forecasting results, we may use a combination of models to obtain a more precise estimate than the one obtained by a single model. In the boosting algorithm, the possible small gain a "weak" model can bring compared to random estimate is boosted by the sequential construction of several such models, which concentrate progressively on the difficult examples of the original training set. Boosting (Schapire, 1990; Freund & Schapire, 1997; Ridgeway et al., 1999) works by sequentially applying a classification algorithm to re-weighted versions of the training data, and then taking a weighted majority vote of the sequence of classifiers thus produced. Freund and Schapire (Freund & Schapire, 1997) presented the Adaboost. R algorithm that attacks the regression problem by reducing it to a classification problem.

A different approach to regressor boosting as residual-fitting was developed in (Duffy & Helmbold, 2002; Buhlmann & Yu 2003). Instead of being trained on a different sample of the same training set, as in previous boosting algorithms, a regressor is trained on a new training set having different target values (e.g. the residual error). Before presenting briefly our algorithm, studied in (Assaad et al, 2005), let us mention that in (Cook & Robinson, 1996) a boosting method is applied to the classification of phonemes, with RNNs as learners. The authors are the first ones to have noticed the implications of the internal memory of the RNNs on the boosting algorithm.

The boosting algorithm employed should comply with the restrictions imposed by the general context of the application. In our case, it must be able to work well when a limited amount of data is available and to accept RNNs as regressors. We followed (Assaad et al, 2008) the generic algorithm of (Freund, 1990). Our updates are based on the suggestion in (Drucker, 1999), but we apply a linear transformation to the weights before we employ them (see the definition of $D_{n+1}(q)$ in Table 1) in order to prevent the RNNs from simply ignoring the easier examples. Then, instead of sampling with replacement according to the updated distribution, we prefer to weight the error computed for each example (thus using all the data points) at the output of the RNN with the distribution value corresponding to the example.

For stage (2a), BPTT equations (14) and (15) become for the output layer:

$$\frac{\partial E(t_1,t_l)}{\partial net_i(\tau)} = \begin{cases} [s_i(t_l) \text{-} d_i(t_l)] D_n(\tau+1) f_i'(net_i(\tau)) & \text{if} \quad i \in T(\tau+1) \\ 0 \quad \text{else} \end{cases} \tag{22}$$

and for the hidden layer:

1. Initialize the weights for the examples: $D_1(q)=1/Q$, and Q, the number of training examples. Put the iteration counter at 0: $n=0$
2. Iterate
   (a) increment n. Learn with BPTT an RNN h_n by using the entire training set and by weighting the squared error computed for example q with $D_n(q)$, the weight of example q for the iteration n;
   (b) update the weights of the examples:
   (i) compute $L_n(q)$ for every $q=1,\cdots,Q$ according to the loss function:
   $L_n^{linear}(q)=\left|y_q^{(n)}(x_q)-y_q\right|/S_n$, $L_n^{quadratic}(q)=\left|y_q^{(n)}(x_q)-y_q\right|^2/S_n^2$
   $L_n^{exponential}(q)=1-\exp\left(-\left|y_q^{(n)}(x_q)-y_q\right|/S_n\right)$, with
   $S_n=\sup_q\left|y_q^{(n)}(x_q)-y_q\right|$;
   (ii) compute $\varepsilon_n=\sum_{q=1}^{Q}D_n(q)L_n(q)$ and $\alpha_n=(1-\varepsilon_n)/\varepsilon_n$;
   (iii) the weights of the examples become (Z_n is a normalizing constant)
   $D_{n+1}(q)=\dfrac{1+k\cdot p_{n+1}(q)}{Q+k}$ with $p_{n+1}(q)=\dfrac{D_n(q)\alpha_n^{(L_n(q)-1)}}{Z_n}$ until $\varepsilon_n<0.5$.
3. Combine RNNs by using the weighted median.

Table 1. The boosting algorithm proposed for regression with recurrent neural networks

$$\frac{\partial E(t_1,t_l)}{\partial net_i(\tau)}=\begin{cases}\left[\begin{array}{l}[s_i(\tau+1)-d_i(\tau+1)]D_n(\tau+1)\\ +\displaystyle\sum_{j\in Succ(i)}\frac{\partial E(t_1,t_l)}{\partial net_j(\tau+1)}w_{ji}(\tau+1)\end{array}\right]f_i'(net_i(\tau)) & \text{if } i\in T(\tau+1)\\ \displaystyle\sum_{j\in Succ(i)}\frac{\partial E(t_1,t_l)}{\partial net_j(\tau+1)}w_{ji}(\tau+1)f_i'(net_i(\tau)) & \text{else}\end{cases} \tag{23}$$

6. Single step ahead prediction results

The results we present here concern univariate regression only, but our algorithms are obviously not limited to such problems. We employed a natural dataset (sunspots) and two synthetic datasets (Mackey-Glass), which allow us to perform comparisons since many related results are published in the literature.

We applied our algorithms to RNNs having an input neuron, a linear output neuron, a bias unit and a recurrent hidden layer composed of neurons with the symmetric sigmoid (tanh) as activation function. We randomly initialized the weights in [-0.3, 0.3]. For the sunspots dataset we tested RNNs having 2 to 15 neurons in the hidden layer and for the Mackey-Glass RNNs having dataset 2 to 8 neurons. Except for boosting, we performed 20 experiments for each architecture. For boosting, we limited the experiments to 5 trial runs for each configuration: (linear, squared or exponential loss functions; value of parameter k), due to heavy calculation time, using the best architecture found by BPTT (12 neurons in the hidden layer for sunspots, 7 neurons for the Mackey-Glass series). We set the maximal number n of RNNs at 50 for each experiment.

In the following we employ the normalized mean square error (NMSE) which is the ratio between the mean square error and the variance of the time series. It is defined, for a time series $x(t)_{t=t_1,\ldots,t_l}$, by

$$\frac{\sum_{t=t_1}^{t_l}\left(x(t)-\hat{x}(t)\right)^2}{\sum_{t=t_1}^{t_l}\left(x(t)-\overline{x}(t)\right)^2}=\frac{\sum_{t=t_1}^{t_l}\left(x(t)-\hat{x}(t)\right)^2}{l\sigma^2} \tag{24}$$

where $\hat{x}(t)$ is the prediction given by the RNN and $\overline{x}(t)$, σ^2 are the mean value and variance estimated from the available data. A value of NMSE=1 is achieved by predicting the unconditional mean of a time series. The normalized root mean squared error (NRMSE) used for some of the results in the literature is the square root of the NMSE.

We compared the results obtained using our algorithms to other results in the literature.

6.1 Sunspots

The sunspots dataset (Fig. 5) is a natural dataset that contains the yearly number of dark spots on the sun from 1700 to 1979. The time series has a pseudo-period of 10 to 11 years. It is common practice to use as the training set the data from 1700 to 1920 and to evaluate the performance of the model on two sets, composed respectively of the data from 1921 to1955 (test1) and of the date from 1956 to 1979 (test2). Test2 is considered to be more difficult.

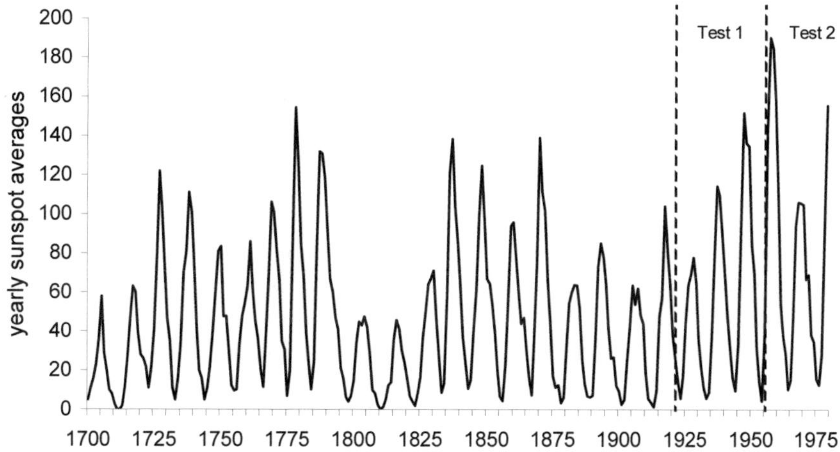

Fig. 5. The sunspots time series

For both CBPTT and EBPTT we set to 20 the upper bound for the delays of the new connections, to 4 the maximal number of new connections and to 20 the number of BPTT iterations performed for each candidate connection during the exploratory stage of EBPTT. Tables 2 and 3 show the NMSE obtained by various models on the two test sets of this benchmark, and the total number of parameters.

Model	Parameters	Test1	Test2
Carbon copy	0	0.427	0.966
TAR	18	**0.097**	**0.280**
MLP Weigend	43	**0.086**	**0.350**
MLP Kouam	43	**0.082**	**0.320**
RNR/BPTT	181	0.102	0.371
RNR/EBPTT 20 it.	15	0.096	0.320
RNR/EBPTT 100 it.	15	0.092	0.308
RNR/CBPTT	15	**0.094**	**0.281**
RNR/Boosting (quad., 20)		0.090	0.296
RNR/Boosting (lin., 10)		**0.082**	**0.314**

Table 2. Mean NMSE obtained by various models on the sunspots time series

Model	Parameters	Test1	Test2
MLP Czernichow	30	**0.078**	**0.283**
TAR	18	0.097	0.280
DRNN1	30	0.091	0.273
DRNN2	45	0.093	0.246
RNN/BPTT	155	0.084	0.300
RNN/EBPTT	23	**0.078**	**0.227**
RNN/CBPTT	15	0.092	0.251
RNN/Delay learning	34	0.081	0.261
RNN/Boosting (quad., 5)		**0.078**	**0.250**
RNN/Boosting (lin., 10)		0.080	0.270

Table 3. Best NMSE obtained by various models

The threshold autoregressive (TAR) model in (Tong & Lim, 1980) employs a threshold to switch between two AR models. The MLP in (Weigend et al., 1991) has a time window of size 12 in the input layer; Table 2 gives the results obtained with weight decay and pruning, which start with 8 hidden neurons and reduce their number to 3. The Dynamical RNNs (DRNNs) are RNNs having FIR connections. We show here the best results obtained in (Aussem, 1999) on each of the two test sets; mean values were not available. DRNN1 has 2 hidden neurons, fully connected by FIR connections of order 5. DRNN2 has 5 hidden neurons, fully connected by FIR connections of order 2. The author found the order of these connections after several trials.

The best result is obtained by EBPTT with 100 iterations, for an RNR with 3 hidden neurons. Constructive algorithms added most of the time 4 connections. For the delay learning algorithm, the experiments show an occasionally unstable behaviour, some learning attempts being soon blocked with high values of error. The internal state of the network (the set of neuron outputs belonging to the hidden layer) happens to be very sensitive to delay variation. The choice of the two learning steps, either for the weights or for connection delays, requires a very precise tuning. The boosting algorithm develops 9 networks with linear and quadratic functions and 36 networks with exponential function.

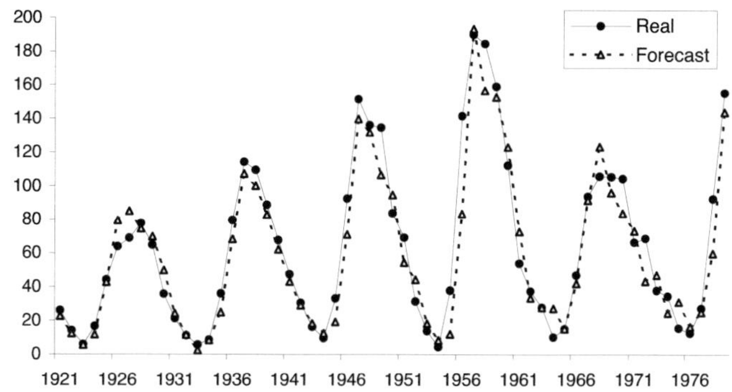

Fig. 6. The predictions obtained with EBPTT on the sunspots test sets

6.2 Mackey-Glass series

The Mackey-Glass benchmarks (Mackey and Glass, 1977) are well-known for the evaluation of SS and MS prediction methods. The time series are generated by the following nonlinear differential equation:

$$\frac{dx}{dt} = -0.1 \cdot x(t) + \frac{0.2 \cdot x(t-\theta)}{1 + x^{10}(t-\theta)} \tag{25}$$

The behavior is chaotic for $\tau > 16{,}8$. The results in the literature usually concern $\tau = 17$ (known as MG17, see Fig. 7) and $\tau = 30$ (MG30). The data is generated and then sampled with a period of 6, according to the common practice, see e.g. (Wan 1993). We use the first 500 values as our learning set and the next 100 values as our test set.

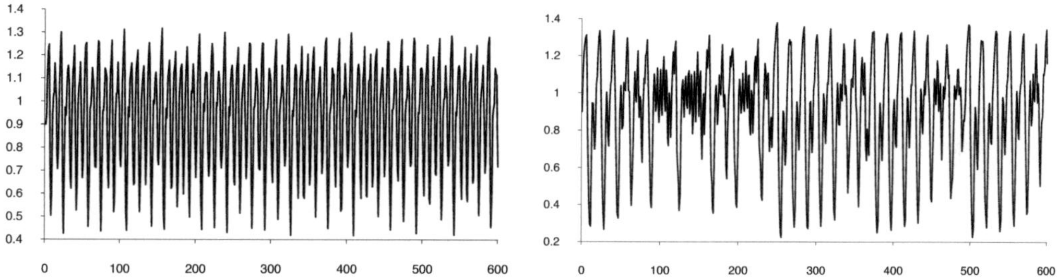

Fig. 7. The Mackey-Glass time series for $\theta = 17$ (left) and $\theta = 30$ (right)

The linear, polynomial, local approaches, RBF and MLP models are mentioned in (Casdagli, 1989). The FIR MLP put forward in (Wan, 1993) has 15 neurons in the hidden layer. FIR connections of order 8 are employed between the inputs and the hidden neurons, while the order of the connections between the hidden neurons and the output is 2. The resulting networks have 196 parameters. The feed-forward network employed in (Duro & Santos Reyes, 1999) consists of a single input neuron, 20 hidden neurons and one output neuron. A delay is associated to every connection in the network, and the value of the delay is modified by a learning algorithm inspired by back-propagation. In (McDonnell & Waagen, 1994) an evolutionary algorithm produces an RNN having 2 hidden neurons with sinusoidal transfer functions and several time-delayed connections.

Model	MG(17)	MG(30)
Linear	269	324
Polynomial	11.2	39.8
Local approach 1	33.1	57.5
Local approach 2	12.9	380.2
RBF	10.7	25.1
FFN	10	31.6
RNN/BPTT	0.99	13.1
RNN/EBPTT	0.62	1.8
RNN/CBPTT	1.66	2.51
Boosting (quad., 100)	**0.16**	**0.45**
Boosting (quad., 200)	**0.18**	**0.45**

Table 4. Mean EQMN (*10^3) obtained by various models on the MG time series

The DRNNs have FIR connections of order 4 between the input and the hidden layer, FIR connections of order 2 between the 4 to 7 hidden neurons, and simple connections to the output neuron (for a total of 197 parameters).
Throughout our experiments, for both EBPTT and CBPTT we set to 34 the maximal value for the delays of the new connections and to 10 the maximal number of new connections. The number of BPTT steps performed for each candidate connection during the exploratory stage of EBPTT was always set to 20; a higher value has a negligible effect here. The mean results reported in Table 4 were obtained with RNNs having 6 hidden neurons, so with 10 time-delayed connections we have a maximum of 65 parameters. The best results were obtained with RNNs having up to 7 hidden neurons, for a maximum of 81 parameters.
Our constructive algorithms significantly improve the results reported in the literature for the two datasets, with regard both to the mean NMSE and to the lowest NMSE. There is also an improvement upon BPTT without the constructive stage.
During our experiments we noticed that the mean value of the delays associated with the new connections was significantly lower for MG(17) than for MG(30). Also, CBPTT added on the average fewer connections than EBPTT. Again, only the first new connections produce a significant reduction in the NMSE.

Model	MG(17)	MG(30)
FIR MLP	4.9	16.2
TDFFN	0.8	
RNN evolutionary algorithm		2.5
DRNN	4.7	7.6
RNRN/BPTT	0.23	0.89
RNN/EBPTT	**0.13**	**0.05**
RNN/CBPTT	0.14	0.73
RNN/delay learning	0.15	
Boosting (lin.,150)	**0.13**	**0.45**
Boosting (quad., 100)	**0.15**	**0.41**

Table 5. Best EQMN (*10^3) obtained by various models on the MG time series

7. Multi step ahead prediction results

While reliable multi-step-ahead (MS) prediction has important applications ranging from system identification to ecological modeling, most of the published literature considers single-step-ahead (SS) time series prediction. The main reason for this is the inherent difficulty of the problems requiring MS prediction and the fact that the results obtained by simple extensions of algorithms developed for SS prediction are often disappointing. Moreover, if many different techniques perform rather similarly on SS prediction problems, significant differences show up when extensions of these techniques are employed on MS problems.

There are several methods for dealing with a MS prediction problem after finding a satisfactory solution to the associated SS problem.

The first and most common method consists in building a predictor for the SS problem and using it recursively for the corresponding MS problem. The estimates provided by the model for the next time step are fed back to the input of the model until the desired prediction horizon is reached. This method is usually called iterated prediction. This simple method is plagued by the accumulation of errors on the difficult data points encountered; the model can quickly diverge from the desired behavior.

A better method consists in training the predictor on the SS problem and, at the same time, in making use of the propagation of penalties across time steps in order to punish the predictor for accumulating errors in MS prediction. This method is called corrected iterated prediction. When the models are MLPs or RNNs, such a procedure is directly inspired from the BPTT algorithm performing gradient descent on the cumulated error. The model is thus simultaneously trained on both the SS and the associated MS prediction problem. Unfortunately, the gradient of the error usually "vanishes" when moving away from the time step during which the penalty was received (Bengio, 1994).

According to the direct method, the predictor is no longer concerned with an SS problem and is directly trained on the MS problem. By a formal analysis of the expected error, it is shown in (Atiya et al., 1999) that the direct method always performs better than the iterated method and at least as well as the corrected iterated method. However, this result relies on several assumptions, among which the ability of the model to perfectly learn the different target functions (the one for SS prediction and the one for direct MS prediction). The results of the learning algorithm may been improved, e.g. when it suffers from the vanishing gradient phenomenon. For instance, improved results were obtained by using recurrent networks and training them with progressively increasing prediction horizons (Suykens & Vandewalle, 1995) or including time-delayed connections from the output of the network to its input (Parlos et al., 2000).

We decided to test on MS prediction problems the previous algorithms that were originally developed for learning long-term dependencies in time series (Boné & al, 2000) or for improving general performance. Constructive algorithms provide a selective addition of time-delayed connections to recurrent networks and were shown to produce parsimonious models (few parameters, linear prior on the longer-range dependencies) with good results on SS prediction problems. These results, together with the fact that a longer-range memory embodied in the time delays should allow a network to better retain the past information when predicting at a long horizon, let us anticipate improved results on MS prediction problems. Some further support for this claim is provided by the experimental evidence in (Parlos et al., 2000) concerning the successful use of time delays in recurrent networks for

MS prediction. We expected the constructive algorithms to identify the most useful delays for a given problem and network architecture, instead of using an entire range of delays.

7.1 Sunspots

All the tested algorithms perform better than standard BPTT and exhibit a fast degradation while simultaneously increasing prediction horizon (Table 6, Fig. 8).

Steps ahead h	Model						
	BPTT	CBPTT	EBPTT	lin. 10	quad. 20	quad. 5	exp. 20
1	0.24	**0.17**	0.19	0.18	**0.17**	0.18	0.18
2	0.88	0.69	0.53	0.43	**0.40**	0.43	0.42
3	1.14	0.99	0.79	**0.54**	**0.54**	0.56	0.67
4	1.22	1.17	0.80	0.67	0.73	**0.64**	0.76
5	1.01	0.99	0.88	0.74	**0.69**	0.73	0.77
6	1.02	1.01	0.84	0.73	0.68	**0.65**	0.74
10	-	-	-	**0.64**	0.69	0.67	0.75
12	-	-	-	0.86	0.97	**0.77**	1.09

Table 6. Best mean NMSE on the sunspots cumulated set (test1+test2) as a function of the prediction horizon

Boosted architectures give the best results. The boosting algorithm develops around 9 weak learners with the linear and quadratic loss functions, and 30 weak learners with the exponential function, as for the SS problem. The mean number of networks remains practically constant while the horizon increases.

If we distinguish between the results on test1 and test2 (not shown here) we can see that the deterioration is mainly due to test2. It is commonly accepted that the behavior on test2 can not be explained (by some longer-range phenomenon) given the available history. Short-range information available in SS prediction lets the network evaluate the rate of change in the number of sunspots. Such information is missing in MS prediction.

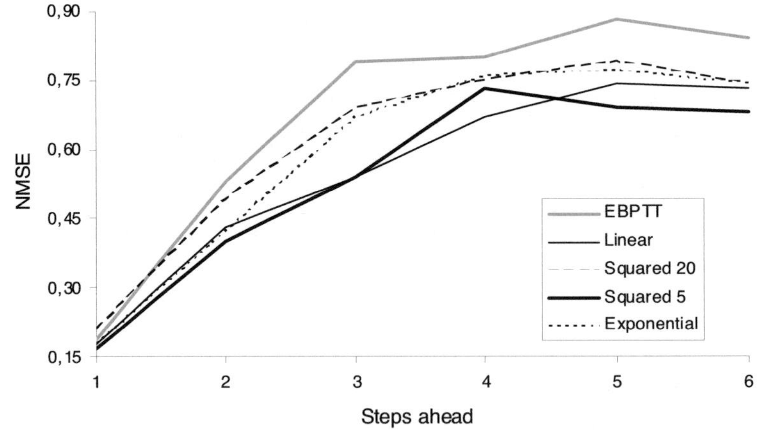

Fig. 8. Sunspots time series: mean NMSE on the cumulated test set as a function of the prediction horizon. Due to their poor results, BPTT and CBPTT algorithms are not represented

7.2 Mackey-Glass series

For the two MG series, we obtained (Tables 7 and 8) around 26 networks with the linear function, 37 with the squared function and between 46 and 50 for the exponential function. The maximal number of networks is set to 50. Tables 7 and 8 show the strong improvements obtained on the original BPTT and on the constructive algorithms.

Steps ahead h	Model					
	BPTT	CBPTT	EBPTT	Lin. 150	quad. 100	exp. 100
1	22	13	1	0.17	**0.16**	0.17
2	179	124	101	**0.24**	0.28	0.25
3	145	124	16	0.57	0.57	**0.52**
4	8	7	4	0.57	0.54	**0.52**
5	266	253	181	**0.98**	1.26	1.27
6	321	321	232	**2.11**	15.2	4.66
10	336	331	219	14.1	**12.2**	15.0
11	289	218	252	**9.80**	12.0	16.8
12	167	156	158	**6.72**	8.66	7.57

Table 7. Best mean results (NMSE*10^3) on MG17 as a function of the prediction horizon

Comparisons with other published results concerning MG17 MS prediction can only be performed for a horizon of 14; the results presented here are inferior to those of the local methods put forward in (Chudy & Farkas 1998; McNames 2000), but for the RNNs trained by our algorithm, significantly fewer data points were employed for training (500 compared to 3000 or 10000), which is the usual benchmark (Casdagli 1989; Wan, 1994). However, the use of a huge number of points for learning the MG17 artificial time series, generated without noise, can lead to models with poor generalization to noisy data.

Steps ahead h	Model					
	BPTT	CBPTT	EBPTT	lin. 300	quad. 200	exp. 150
1	11.7	2.5	1.8	**0.45**	**0.45**	0.47
2	19.9	9.7	3.3	0.49	**0.48**	0.59
3	4	2.2	1.6	0.56	**0.55**	0.64
4	2.2	2.1	1.6	0.47	**0.43**	0.48
5	2.6	2.3	0.9	0.85	**0.67**	0.72
6	8.9	8.3	6.4	**1.75**	1.92	1.80
7	70.1	65.6	64.3	2.98	4.56	**2.72**
8	336	203	112	**5.08**	109	57.0
9	801	379	257	84.0	276	**3.71**
10	892	383	73.7	2.79	204	**2.63**
11	411	230	285	**6.34**	21.3	8.05

Table 8. Best mean results (NMSE*10^3) on MG30 as a function of the prediction horizon

8. Conclusion

Adding time-delayed connections to recurrent neural networks helps gradient descent algorithms in learning medium or long-term dependencies. However, by systematically adding finite impulse response connections, one obtains oversized networks which are slow to train and need regularization techniques in order to improve generalization. We apply here two constructive approaches, which starts with a RNN having no time-delayed connections and progressively adds some, an approach based on a particular type of neuron whose connections have a real value and adapted to recurrent networks and a boosting algorithm. The experimental results we obtained on three benchmark problems show that by adding only a few time-delayed connections we are able to produce networks having comparatively few parameters and good performance for SS problems.

The results show also that boosting recurrent neural networks improve strongly MS forecasting. The boosting effect proved to be less effective for sunspots MS forecasts because some short-term dependencies are essential for the prediction of some parts of the data. The fact that for the Mackey-Glass datasets the results are better on the most difficult of the two sets (MG30) can be explained by noticing that long-range dependencies play a more important role for MG30 than for MG17.

9. References

Assaad, M.; Boné, R. & Cardot, H. (2005). Study of the Behavior of a New Boosting Algorithm for Recurrent Neural Networks, *Proceeding of Int. Conference on Artificial Neural Networks*, LNCS, Vol. 3697, 169-174, Warsaw, Poland, Springer-Verlag

Assaad, M.; Boné, R. & Cardot, H. (2008). A New Boosting Algorithm for Improved Time-Series Forecasting with Recurrent Neural Networks, *Information Fusion*, Vol. 9, No. 1, January 2008, 41-55

Atiya, A. F.; El-Shoura, S. M.; Shaheen, S. I. & El-Sherif, M. S. (1999). A Comparison Between Neural Network Forecasting Techniques - Case Study: River Flow Forecasting. *IEEE Transactions on Neural Networks*, Vol. 10, No. 2, 402-409.

Aussem, A. (1999). Dynamical Recurrent Neural Networks: Towards Prediction and Modelling of Dynamical Systems, *Neurocomputing*, Vol. 28, 207-232

Aussem, A. (2002). Sufficient Conditions for Error Backflow Convergence in Dynamical Recurrent Neural Networks, *Neural Computation*, Vol. 14, No. 8, 1907-1927.

Bengio, Y.; Simard, P. & Frasconi, P. (1994). Learning Long-Term Dependencies with Gradient Descent is Difficult, *IEEE Transactions on Neural Networks*, Vol. 5, No. 2, 157-166

Boné, R.; Crucianu, M. & Asselin de Beauville, J.-P. (2000a). An Algorithm for the Addition of Time-Delayed Connections to Recurrent Neural Networks, *Proceedings of European Symposium on Artificial Neural Networks*, pp. 293-298, Bruges, Belgium

Boné, R.; Crucianu, M.; Verley, G. & Asselin de Beauville, J.-P. (2000b). A Bounded Exploration Approach to Constructive Algorithms for Recurrent Neural Networks, *Proceedings of International Joint Conference on Neural Networks*, Vol. 3, pp. 27-32, Como, Italy

Boné, R.; Crucianu, M. & Asselin de Beauville, J.-P. (2002). Learning Long Term Dependencies by the Selective Addition of Time-Delayed Connections to Recurrent Neural Networks, *NeuroComputing*, Vol 48, 251-266

Bühlmann, P. & Yu, B. (2003). Boosting with L2-loss: Regression and Classification, *Journal of the American Statistical Association*, Vol. 98 , 324-340

Campolucci, P.; Uncini, A.; Piazza, F. & Rao, B. D. (1999). On-line learning algorithms for locally recurrent neural networks. *IEEE Transaction on Neural Networks*, Vol. 10, No. 2, 253-271

Casdagli, M. (1989). Nonlinear Prediction of Chaotic Time Series, *Physica*, Vol. 35D , 335-356.

Chudy, L. & Farkas, I. (1998). Prediction of Chaotic Time-Series Using Dynamic Cell Structures and Local Linear Models. *Neural Network World*, Vol. 8, 481-489

Cook, G.D. & Robinson, A.J. (1996). Boosting the Performance of Connectionist Large Vocabulary Speech Recognition, *Proceedings of International Conference in Spoken Language Processing*, pp. 1305-1308, Philadelphia, PA

Czernichow, T.; Piras, A.; Imhof, K.; Caire, P.; Jaccard, Y.; Dorizzi, B. & Germont, A. (1996) Short Term Electrical Load Forecasting with Artificial Neural Networks, *Engineering Intelligent Systems*, Vol. 4, No. 2, 85-99

Drucker, H. (1999). Boosting Using Neural Nets, In *Combining Artificial Neural Nets: Ensemble and Modular Learning*, A. Sharkey, (Ed.), 51-77, Springer

Duffy, N. & Helmbold, D. (2002). Boosting Methods for Regression, *Machine Learning*, Vol. 47, 153-200

Duro, R.J. & Santos Reyes, J. (1999). Discrete-Time Backpropagation for Training Synaptic Delay-Based Artificial Neural Networks. *IEEE Transactions on Neural Networks*, Vol. 10, No. 4, 779-789.

El Hihi, S. & Bengio, Y. (1996). Hierarchical Recurrent Neural Networks for Long-Term Dependencies, *Advances in Neural Information Processing Systems VIII*, M. Mozer, D. S. Touretzky and M. Perrone, (Eds), 493-499, MIT Press, Cambridge, MA

Frasconi, P. ; Gori, M. & Soda, G. (1992). Local Feedback Mulitlayered Networks. *Neural Computation*, Vol. 4, No. 1, 120-130

Freund, Y. (1990,). Boosting a Weak Learning Algorithm by Majority, *Proceedings of Workshop on Computational Learning Theory*, pp. 202-216

Freund, Y. 1 Schapire, R.E. (1997). A Decision-Theoretic Generalization of On-Line Learning and an Application to Boosting. *Journal of Computer and System Sciences*, Vol. 55, 119-139

Guignot, J. & Gallinari, P. (1994). Recurrent Neural Networks with Delays, *Proceedings of International Conference on Artificial Neural Networks*, pp. 389-392, Sorrento

Hammer, B. & Tino, P. (2003). Recurrent Neural Networks with Small Weights Implement Definite Memory Machines, *Neural Computation*, Vol. 15, No. 8, 1897-1926

Hochreiter, S. & Schmidhuber, J. (1997). Long Short-Term Memory. *Neural Computation*, Vol. 9, No. 8, 1735-1780

Lin, T.; Horne, B.G.; Tino, P. & Giles, C.L. (1996). Learning Long-Term Dependencies in NARX Recurrent Neural Networks. *IEEE Transactions on Neural Networks*, Vol.7, No. 6, 1329-1338

McNames, J. (2000). Local Modeling Optimization for Time Series Prediction. *Proceedings of 8th European Symposium on Artificial Neural Networks*, pp. 305-310, Bruges, Belgium

Mackey, M. & Glass, L. (1977). Oscillations and Chaos in Physiological Control Systems, *Science*, 197-287

Parlos, A.G.; Rais, O.T. & Atiya, A.F (2000). Multi-Step-Ahead Prediction Using Dynamic Recurrent Neural Networks. *Neural Networks*, Vol. 13, 765-786

Pearlmutter, B.A. (1990). Dynamic Recurrent Neural Networks. *Research Report CMU-CS-90-196*. Carnegie Mellon University.

Schapire, R.E. (1990). The Strength of Weak Learnability, *Machine Learning*, Vol. 5, 197-227.

Seidl, D.R. & Lorenz, R.D. (1991). A Structure by which a Recurrent Neural Network Can Approximate a Nonlinear Dynamic System, Proceedings of *International Joint Conference on Neural Networks*, pp. 709-714.

Siegelmann, H.T.; Horne, B.G. & Giles C.L. (1997). Computational Capabilities of Recurrent NARX Neural Networks. *IEEE Transactions on Systems, Man and Cybernetics*, Vol. 27, No. 2, 209-214

Suykens, J.A.K. & Vandewalle, J. (1995). Learning a Simple Recurrent Neural State Space Model to Behave Like Chua's Double Scroll. *IEEE Transactions on Circuits and Systems-I*, Vol. 42, 499-502

Takens, F. (1981). Detecting Strange Attractors in Turbulence. *Dynamical Systems and Turbulence*. Dynamical Systems and Turbulence, Lecture Notes in Mathematics, Vol. 898, 366–381, Springer-Verlag, Berlin

Tong, H. & Lim, K.S. (1980). Threshold Autoregression, Limit Cycles and Cyclical Data, *Journal of the Royal Statistical Society*, Vol. B42 , 245-292

Tsoi, A.C. & Back, A.D. (1994). Locally Recurrent Globally Feedforward Networks: A Critical Review of Architectures. *IEEE Transactions on Neural Networks*, Vol. 5, No 2, 229-239

Wan, E. A. (1993). Finite Impulse Response Neural Networks with Applications in Time Series Prediction, PhD Thesis, Stanford University, 140p

Wan, E.A. (1994). Time Series Prediction by Using a Connection Network with Internal Delay Lines, In: *Time Series Prediction: Forecasting the Future and Understanding the Past*, A. S. Weigend and N. A. Gershenfeld, (Eds), 195-217, Addison-Wesley

Weigend, A.S.; Rumelhart, D.E. & Huberman, B.A. (1991). Generalization by Weight-Elimination applied to Currency Exchange Rate Prediction, Proceedings of *International Joint Conference on Neural Networks*, pp. 837-841, Seattle, USA

3

A New Application of Recurrent Neural Networks for EMG-Based Diagnosis of Carpal Tunnel Syndrome

Konuralp Ilbay[1*], Elif Derya Übeyli[2], Gul Ilbay[3], Faik Budak[4]
[1]*Kocaeli University, Faculty of Medicine, Department of Neurosurgery, Kocaeli,*
[2]*Osmaniye Korkut Ata University, Faculty of Engineering, Department of Electrical and Electronics Engineering, Osmaniye,*
[3]*Kocaeli University, Faculty of Medicine, Department of Physiology, Kocaeli,*
[4]*Kocaeli University, Faculty of Medicine, Department of Neurology, Kocaeli, Turkey*

1. Introduction

Carpal tunnel syndrome (CTS), an entrapment neuropathy of median nerve at the wrist, is one of the most common peripheral nerve disorders with an incidence of 99 per 100.000 population (Bland JDP, 2005., Sternbach G, 1999). CTS is more common in females than males, with a ratio of seven to three. Although it is more prevelent between the fourth and sixth decades, it occurs in all age groups (Kanaan N & Sawaya RA, 2001). The condition produces bilateral symptoms in approximately half of patients (von Schroeder HP & Motte MJ, 1996), but dominant hand usually is more severely affected, especially in idiopathic cases (Ilbay K et al.,2010, Preston DC & Shapiro BE, 2005).

CTS arises from compression of the median nerve between the transverse carpal ligament, also called the flexor retinaculum, superiorly, and the flexor tendons, and carpal bones inferiorly. Anatomically, the fibres of median nerve originate from the fifth, sixth, seventh, and eighth cervical roots, and the first thoracic root and pass through the lateral and medial cords of the brachial plexus. The motor branch innervates the abductor pollicis brevis, opponens pollicis, and the two lateral lumbricals in the hand. The sensory branch supplies sensation to the volar aspect of the radial three digits and the lateral half of the fourth digit extending to the palm and the distal dorsal aspects of these digits beyond the distal interphalangeal joints (Kanaan N & Sawaya RA, 2001).

There are two distinct varieties of CTS-acute and chronic. The acute form is relatively uncommon condition in which there is a rapid and sustained rise in interstitial pressure in the carpal tunnel. This most commonly occurs as the result of a distal radius fracture as described by Sir James Paget (Sternbach G, 1999). Other causes include burns, rheumatoid arthritis, infections, haemorrhage (caused by coagulopathy or trauma), repetitive and intensive manual work and injection injuries (Table 1) (Sternbach G, 1999., Aroori S & Spence RAJ, 2008., Luchetti R, 2007).

* Corresponding authore-mail: konuralpilbay@yahoo.com

Burns
Wrist fracture and dislocation
Haemorrhage
Infections
Injection injuries
Rheumatoid arthritis
Repetitive and intensive manual work

Table 1. Acute CTS causes

The chronic form is much more common and symptoms can persist for months to years. However, in only 50 % of cases are the cause identified (Aroori S & Spence RAJ, 2008). The causes of chronic CTS summarised in Table 2.

Any process that increases the volume of the contents of the carpal tunnel, such as tumour, inflammation, and edema, will elevate the pressure within the canal (Sternbach G, 1999). The pathophysiological mechanism of the nerve lesion is ischemic with the compression of the vasa nervosum secondary to the increased pressure (Sunderland S, 1976).

In most patients, the cause of CTS is not clear and it is defined as idiopathic. The idiopathic forms frequently show up as "non specific tenosynovitis" (Sternbach G, 1999., Luchetti R, 2007).

Patients with CTS may present with a variety of symptoms and signs. In early stages, patients usually complain of aching, burning, tingling or numb sensations in the distribution of median nerve distal to wrist. The portion of the hand involved is typically the thumb, index and middle fingers, and radial half of the ring finger. Symptoms are typically worse at night, are exaggerated by a flexed or extended wrist posture (Kanaan N & Sawaya RA, 2001., Preston DC & Shapiro BE, 2005). The pain may radiate to the forearm, arm, or rarely shoulder. Motor complaints include finger weakness and the disease may be mistaken for cervical radiculopathy, shoulder bursitis, thoracic outlet syndrome, transient ischemic attack, coronary artery ischemia, tendinitis, fibrositis or lateral epicondylitis. Long-term involvement leads to thenar muscle atrophy, with loss of thumb abduction and opposition strength (Sternbach G, 1999., Kanaan N & Sawaya RA, 2001).

The diagnosis of CTS based mainly on clinical symptoms and nerve conduction studies. Imaging studies have played a minimal role in evaluation of CTS. Magnetic resonance imaging (MRI) has recently been shown to help in establishing the diagnosis. But the application of MRI in CTS diagnosis has been limited and should remain so for reasons: 1) routine electrophysiologic studies are adequate and can be performed with confidence in both community and academic settings; 2) MRI remains expensive; 3) acquisition of high-quality peripheral nerve images and their expert interpretation is not widely available; and 4) the low specifity of MRI could complicate treatment decision (Fleckenstein JL & Wolfe GI, 2002).

High-resolution ultrasound has advantages over MRI in terms of cost and provides dynamic images. It has been shown to produce accurate measurements of carpal tunnel and nerve diameters (Kamolz LP et al, 2001).

This chapter presents the use of recurrent neural networks (RNNs) for diagnosis of CTS. In different disciplines for modelling complex real-world problems, artificial neural networks (ANNs) have many applications. ANNs have been used for solution of different problems, such as pattern classification, time series prediction, nonlinear control, function approximation, and biomedical signals analysis. ANNs can produce nonlinear models

A.Local and regional causes	B.Systemic causes
Tumours	Diabetes
	Alcohol
Ganglion	Obesity
Haemangioma	Hypothyroidism
Cyst	Pregnancy
Lipoma	Menopause
Neuroma	Systemic lupus erythematosus
	Dermatomyositis
Anatomical anomalies	Scleroderma
Bony abnormalities	Renal failure
Abnormal muscle bellies	Long-term haemodialysis
Persistent median artery	Acromegaly
Aneurysm or arterio-venous malformation	Multiple myeloma
	Sarcoidosis
Inflammatory	
Tenosynovitis	
Hypertrophic synovium	
Histoplasma fungal infection	
Gout	
Amyloidosis	

Table 2. Causes of chronic form of CTS

relating the inputs (the independent variables of a system) to the outputs (the dependent predictive variables). ANNs are desirable because learning and adaptivity allow the system to modify its internal structure in response to changing environment and the model can be applied to the unlearned data. RNNs have a wide application field among the ANNs architectures. One of the most important applications of pattern recognition is automated diagnostic systems and they have role at assisting doctors in making diagnostic decisions (Haykin S, 1994; Basheer I.A. & Hajmeer M., 2000; Chaudhuri B.B. & Bhattacharya U., 2000; Miller A.S. et al., 1992).

The recurrent neural networks (RNNs) (Elman J.L., 1990; Thissen U. et al., 2003; Übeyli E.D., 2008a; 2008b; 2009a; 2009b; Übeyli E.D. & Übeyli M., 2008; Ilbay K et al., 2010) have been studied extensively for classification, regression and density estimation. The results of the existing studies (Elman J.L., 1990; Thissen U. et al., 2003; Übeyli E.D., 2008a; 2008b; 2009a; 2009b; Übeyli E.D. & Übeyli M., 2008; Ilbay K et al., 2010) showed that the RNNs have high accuracy in classification of the biomedical data, therefore we used the RNNs in the diagnosis of CTS. In this study, in order to diagnose CTS, the RNNs and multilayer perceptron neural network (MLPNN) trained with the Levenberg-Marquardt algorithm are implemented (Figure 1). A significant contribution of the present chapter is to examine the performance of the RNNs on the diagnosis of CTS (normal, right CTS, left CTS, bilateral CTS).

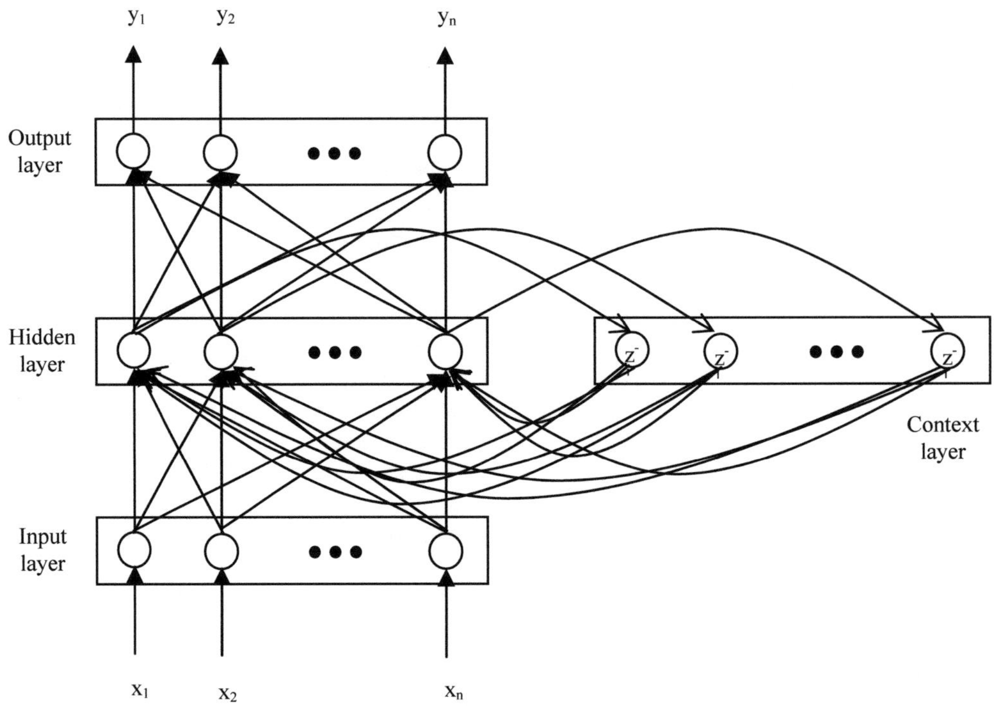

Fig. 1. A schematic representation of an Elman recurrent neural network. z^{-1} represents a one time step delay unit (Thissen U. et al., 2003).

2. Electrophysiological tests for the diagnosis of CTS: nerve conduction study and electromyography

The combination of clinical symptoms and signs with electrodiagnostic findings allows possible prognostic validation for the neurosurgeon. Neurophysiology is a method that solely expresses the functional state of the median nerve alone with carpal tunnel (Haase J, 2001).

The usual electrophysiological procedures start with nerve conduction studies (NCS), sensory followed by motor NCS. Next, electromyography (EMG) is performed (Cornblath DR & Chaudry V, 2001).

NCS are based on the principle of nerve stimulation across the area of interest. For median nerve, the nerve is stimulated proximal to the carpal ligament and compound muscle action potential (CMAP) is picked up by skin electrodes placed over the thenar eminence. The CMAP reflects the status of the motor fibres in the median nerve. The amplitude of the CMAP reveals stimulation of the whole population of motor nerve fibres. The duration reflects the conduction velocities across the different fibres. The latency, between the point of nerve stimulation and the onset of the CMAP, reveals the fastest velocity of the motor fibres across the carpal tunnel (Kanaan N & Sawaya RA, 2001).

The sensory component of the median nerve is affected much earlier than the motor component and in early stages of CTS there is usually a delay in the sensory nerve conduction study. Stimulation of sensory fibres is done at the same location as for motor stimulation and the sensory nerve action potential is recorded from the distal phalange of the second or third digits. The study of the sensory fibres can be performed orthodromically or anti-dromically (Kanaan N & Sawaya RA, 2001., Aroori S & Spence RAJ, 2008).

Those studies usually involve a comparison of the median nerve to another nerve in the same hand. The ulnar nerve is the nerve most commonly used for comparison (Preston DC & Shapiro BE, 2005).

Needle electromyography (EMG) is a complementary rather than a compulsory test in addition to NCS. EMG describes the functional state of the muscle fibres that are dependent on innervation by motor axons. In CTS, it is usually performed on the median nerve - innervated muscles of the hand and forearm. Denervation activity in the EMG reflects recent nerve damage. Neurogenic changes and reinnervation potentials indicate chronic nerve pathology (Kanaan N & Sawaya RA, 2001). Following of nerve decompression, a typical reiinervation pattern is found often earlier than that by clinical examination (Haase J, 2007).

EMG is also used to reveal other nerve lesions in the involved arm when the findings of NCS are not consistent with CTS. These include nerve entrapment in the forearm, plexus lesions or cervical root disease (Kanaan N & Sawaya RA, 2001).

3. Database description and evaluation of electrophysiologic recordings

We retrospectively considered 350 patients (289 females and 61 males) with various CTS symptoms and signs who underwent nerve conduction studies. Of these patients, 121 had no electrophysiologic evidence of CTS, and were accepted as normal group (103 females and 18 males). 229 of the patients were suffered from right CTS (32 females and 15 males), left CTS (22 females and 14 males) and bilateral CTS (132 females and 14 males). Patients with generalized peripheral neuropathy caused by diabetes or other medical illness and those who had undergone prior carpal tunnel surgery were not included in the study. Each subject completed a self-administered questionnaire. The questionnaire focused on hand symptoms that are commonly associated with CTS.

All the studies were performed with the subjects at supine position in a warm room with the temperature maintained at 26 to 28°C. Skin temperatures were checked over the forearm. Nerve conduction studies were performed using standard techniques of supramaximal percutaneous stimulation with a constant current stimulator and surface electrode recording on both hands of each subject. Sensory responses were obtained antidromically stimulating at the wrist and recording from the index finger (median nerve) or little finger (ulnar nerve), with ring electrodes at a distance of 14 cm. The results of the median motor nerve obtained by stimulating the median motor nerve at the wrist and elbow and the recording was done over the abductor pollicis brevis muscle. The results of the ulnar motor nerve were performed by stimulating the ulnar nerve at the wrist, below the elbow, and above the elbow and the recording was done over the abductor digiti minimi muscle, with the arm flexed 135°. In the present study, the following median nerve and ulnar nerve measures were used: (1) distal onset latency of the sensory nerve action potential (DL-S); (2) distal onset latency of the compound muscle action potential (DL-M). Median sensory latency greater than 3.5 ms, median motor latency greater than 4.2 ms was used as the criteria for abnormal median nerve conduction (Budak F et al., 2001).

4. Recurrent Neural Networks

In the diagnosis applications, Elman RNNs were used and therefore the Elman RNN is presented in this chapter. In principle, the set up of an Elman RNN is formed as a regular feedforward network. In the architecture of the network, all neurons in one layer are connected with all neurons in the next layer. The only difference in the architecture of the Elman RNN is the context layer which is a special case of a hidden layer. The neurons in the context layer, which are called as context neurons, hold a copy of the output of the hidden neurons. The output of each hidden neuron is copied into a specific neuron in the context layer. The value of the context neuron is used as an extra input signal for all the neurons in the hidden layer one time step later. Therefore, the Elman network has an explicit memory of one time lag (Elman J.L., 1990; Thissen U. et al., 2003).

The strength of all connections between neurons are denoted with a weight. Initially, all weight values are chosen randomly and are optimized during the stage of training. In an Elman network, the weights from the hidden layer to the context layer are set to one and are fixed because the values of the context neurons have to be copied exactly. After this stage, the initial output weights of the context neurons are equal to half the output range of the other neurons in the network. The training algorithms of the Elman network are similar to the training algorithms of the regular feedforward neural networks. So, the Elman network can be trained with gradient descent backpropagation and optimization methods (Thissen U. et al., 2003; Pineda F.J., 1987). In the many applications, the backpropagation has some problems. The algorithm cannot find the global minimum of the error function, because gradient descent can probably get stuck in local minima, where it may remain indefinitely. Therefore, in order to improve the convergence of the backpropagation a lot of variations were proposed (Haykin S., 1994). In the training of neural networks optimization methods such as second-order methods (conjugate gradient, quasi-Newton, Levenberg-Marquardt) have also been used. The Levenberg-Marquardt algorithm combines the best features of the Gauss-Newton technique and the steepest-descent algorithm and omitted their limitations. The algorithm suffers from the problem of slow convergence (Battiti R., 1992; Hagan M.T. & Menhaj M.B., 1994) and can obtain a good cost function compared with the other training algorithms.

The Levenberg-Marquardt algorithm is a least-squares estimation algorithm based on the maximum neighborhood. $E(\mathbf{w})$ be an objective error function composed of m individual error terms $e_i^2(\mathbf{w})$ as follows:

$$E(\mathbf{w}) = \sum_{i=1}^{m} e_i^2(\mathbf{w}) = \|f(\mathbf{w})\|^2, \tag{1}$$

where $e_i^2(\mathbf{w}) = (\mathbf{y}_{di} - \mathbf{y}_i)^2$ and $\mathbf{y}_{di}$ is the desired value of output neuron i, $\mathbf{y}_i$ is the actual output of that neuron.

It is assumed that function $f(\cdot)$ and its Jacobian J are known at point $\mathbf{w}$. The Levenberg-Marquardt algorithm is trying to compute the weight vector $\mathbf{w}$ such that $E(\mathbf{w})$ is minimum. Then by the Levenberg-Marquardt algorithm, a new weight vector $\mathbf{w}_{k+1}$ can be computed from the previous weight vector $\mathbf{w}_k$ as follows:

$$\mathbf{w}_{k+1} = \mathbf{w}_k + \delta\mathbf{w}_k, \tag{2}$$

where $\delta \mathbf{w}_k$ is defined as

$$\delta \mathbf{w}_k = -(J_k{}^T f(\mathbf{w}_k))(J_k{}^T J_k + \lambda \mathbf{I})^{-1}. \tag{3}$$

In equation (3), J_k is the Jacobian of f computed at $\mathbf{w}_k$, λ is the Marquardt parameter, $\mathbf{I}$ is the identity matrix (Battiti R., 1992; Hagan M.T. & Menhaj M.B., 1994). The Levenberg-Marquardt algorithm can be explained as in the following:

i. compute $E(\mathbf{w}_k)$,
ii. start with a small value of λ ($\lambda = 0.01$),
iii. solve equation (3) for $\delta \mathbf{w}_k$ and compute $E(\mathbf{w}_k + \delta \mathbf{w}_k)$,
iv. if $E(\mathbf{w}_k + \delta \mathbf{w}_k) \geq E(\mathbf{w}_k)$, increase λ by a factor of 10 and go to (iii),
v. if $E(\mathbf{w}_k + \delta \mathbf{w}_k) < E(\mathbf{w}_k)$, decrease λ by a factor of 10, update $\mathbf{w}_k : \mathbf{w}_k \leftarrow \mathbf{w}_k + \delta \mathbf{w}_k$ and go to (iii).

5. Results and discussion

In this application example, the inputs of the RNNs are the features of CTS (right median motor latency, left median motor latency, right median sensory latency, left median sensory latency). Tables 3 and 4 (Ilbay K et al., 2010) show the values including right median motor latency, left median motor latency, right median sensory latency, left median sensory latency (four features used as inputs of the classifiers) of sample records of two classes (bilateral CTS and normal) which are presented in reports of the subjects.

Motor Nerve Conduction Study

Site	Latency (ms)	Amplitude	Area	Segment	Distance (mm)	Interval (ms)	NCV (m/s)
Median, L							
Wrist	4,74ms	7,83mV	16,09mVms	Wrist		4,74ms	
Elbow	8,25ms	6,68mV	13,43mVms	Wrist- Elbow	170mm	3,51ms	48,4m/s
Median,R							
Wrist	6,42ms	6,77mV	15,66mVms	Wrist		6,42ms	
Elbow	10,26ms	5,24mV	11,94mVms	Wrist- Elbow	170mm	3,84ms	44,3m/s
Ulnar, R							
Wrist	2,85ms	18,22mV	29,78mVms	Wrist		2,85ms	
Elbow	5,91ms	17,77mV	29,36mVms	Wrist- Elbow	180mm	3,06ms	58,8m/s

Sensory Nerve Conduction Study

Site	Latency (ms)	Amplitude	Area	Segment	Distance (mm)	Interval (ms)	NCV (m/s)
Median, L							
Wrist	4,32ms	19,60uV	1,24uVms	Wrist		4,32ms	
Median,R							
Wrist	4,72ms	7,20uV	1,00uVms	Wrist		4,72ms	
Ulnar, R							
Wrist	2,58ms	31,60uV	1,28uVms	Wrist		2,58ms	

Table 3. Values of median motor and sensory latency of the conduction study of the patient with bilateral CTS (Ilbay K et al., 2010).

The samples of the electromyogram (EMG) records of the patient with bilateral CTS and the normal subject are shown in Figures 2 and 3 (Ilbay K et al., 2010). MATLAB software package (MATLAB version 7.0 with neural networks toolbox) was used for implementation of the RNN and the MLPNN. The determination of architecture and training are important for the neural networks used in classification. The sizes of the training set and test set are determining the efficiency of neural networks. In order to determine the sizes of the training and testing sets of the CTS database, various experiments were performed. In the developed classifiers, 100 of 350 records were used for training and the rest for testing. The training set consisted of 40 normal, 17 right CTS, 12 left CTS and 31 bilateral CTS. The testing set consisted of 81 normal, 30 right CTS, 24 left CTS and 115 bilateral CTS (Ilbay K et al., 2010).

Motor Nerve Conduction Study

Site	Latency (ms)	Amplitude	Area	Segment	Distance (mm)	Interval (ms)	NCV (m/s)
Median, L							
Wrist	3,92ms	10,91mV	17,95mVms	Wrist		3,92ms	
Elbow	7,76ms	12,32mV	20,40mVms	Wrist- Elbow	220mm	3,81ms	57,7m/s
Median,R							
Wrist	3,72ms	2,70mV	64,21mVms	Wrist		3,72ms	
Elbow	8,04ms	3,38mV	51,41mVms	Wrist- Elbow	250mm	4,32ms	57,9m/s
Ulnar, R							
Wrist	2,58ms	4,07mV	3,51mVms	Wrist		2,85ms	
Elbow	6,72ms	3,31mV	2,64mVms	Wrist- Elbow	240mm	4,14ms	58,0m/s

Sensory Nerve Conduction Study

Site	Latency (ms)	Amplitude	Area	Segment	Distance (mm)	Interval (ms)	NCV (m/s)
Median, L							
Wrist	2,64ms	36,60uV	3,25uVms	Wrist		2,64ms	
Median,R							
Wrist	2,76ms	11,60uV	1,82uVms	Wrist		2,66ms	
Ulnar, R							
Wrist	2,58ms	25,90uV	1,28uVms	Wrist		2,36ms	

Table 4. Values of median motor and sensory latency of the conduction study of the normal subject (Ilbay K et al., 2010).

In the determination of efficient neural network architecture, experiments were done for different network architectures and the results of the architecture studies confirmed that networks with one hidden layer consisting of 25 recurrent neurons results in higher classification accuracy. In order to compare performance of the different classifiers, for the same classification problem MLPNN which is the most commonly used feedforward neural networks was implemented. The single hidden layered (20 hidden neurons) MLPNN was used to classify the CTS. The sigmoidal function was used as the activation function in the hidden layer and the output layer.

The confusion matrices are used to display the classification results of the classifiers. In a confusion matrix, each cell contains the raw number of exemplars classified for the corresponding combination of desired and actual network outputs. The confusion matrices showing the classification results of the classifiers used for classification of the CTS are given in Table 5 (Ilbay K et al., 2010). From these matrices one can tell the frequency with which record is misclassified as another. The test performance of the classifiers can be determined by the computation of sensitivity, specificity and total classification accuracy. The sensitivity, specificity and total classification accuracy are defined as:

Sensitivity: number of true positive decisions / number of actually positive cases

Specificity: number of true negative decisions / number of actually negative cases

Total classification accuracy: number of correct decisions / total number of cases

A true negative decision occurs when both the classifier and the physician suggested the absence of a positive detection. A true positive decision occurs when the positive detection of the classifier coincided with a positive detection of the physician.

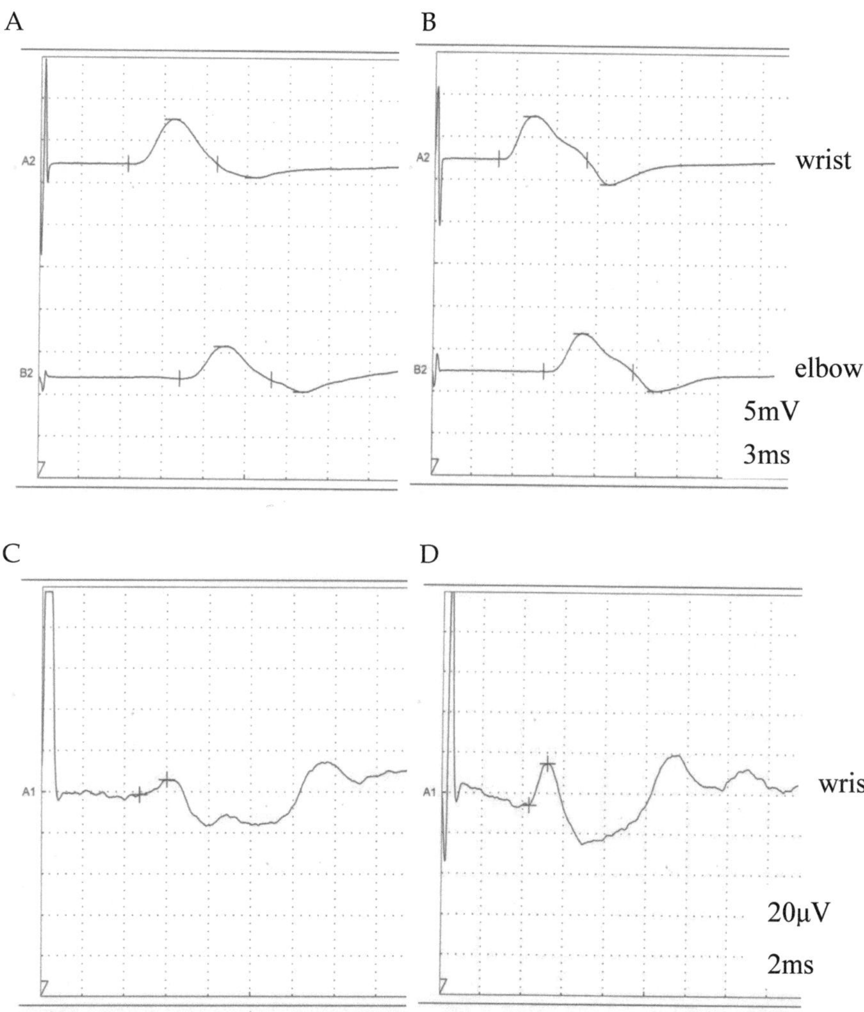

Fig. 2. The samples of EMG records of the patient with bilateral CTS; **A**. Image of motor nerve conduction study of right median nerve, **B**. Image of motor nerve conduction study of left median nerve, **C**. Image of sensory nerve conduction study of right median nerve, **D**. Image of sensory nerve conduction study of left median nerve (Ilbay K et al., 2010).

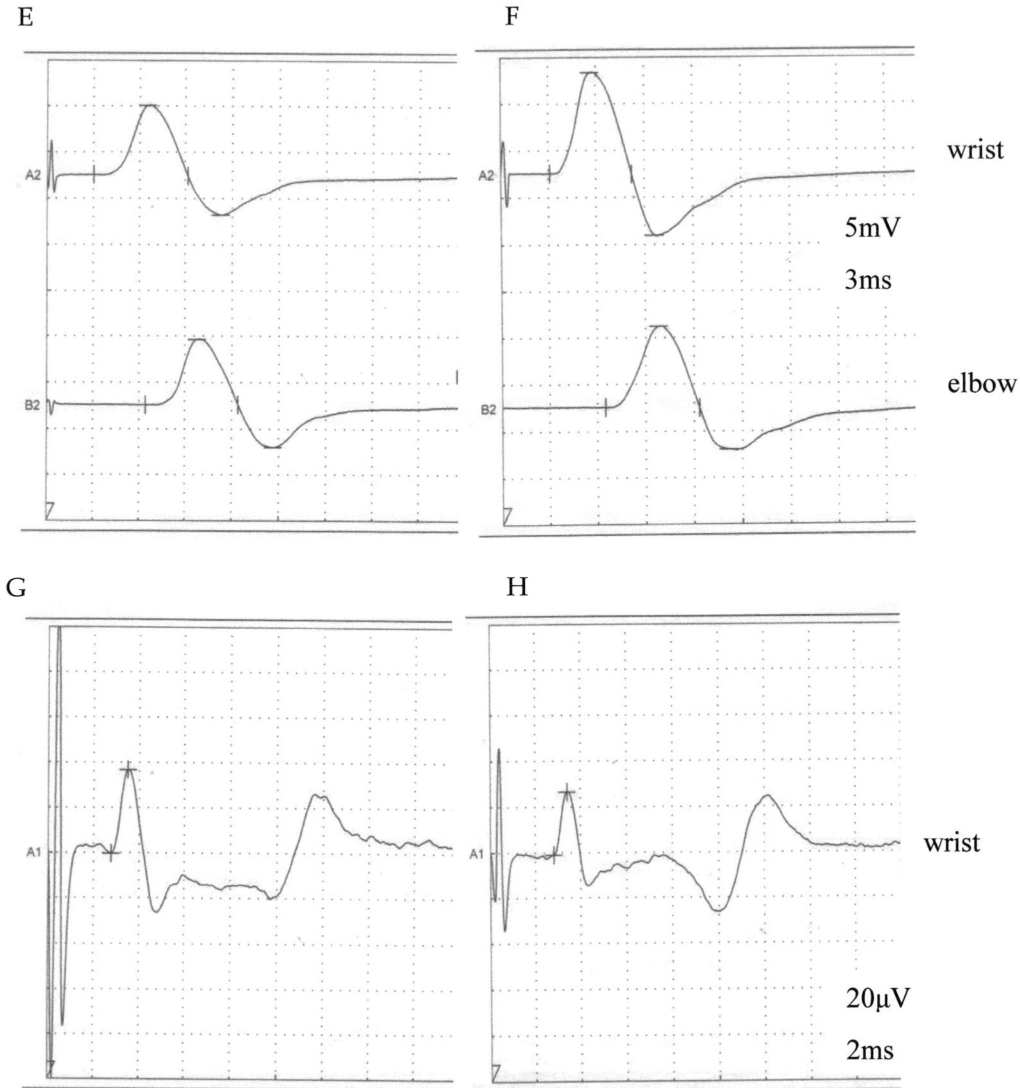

Fig. 3. The samples of EMG records of the normal subject; **E.** Image of motor nerve conduction study of right median nerve, **F.** Image of motor nerve conduction study of left median nerve, **G.** Image of sensory nerve conduction study of right median nerve, **H.** Image of sensory nerve conduction study of left median nerve (Ilbay K et al., 2010).

The classification accuracies (specificity, sensitivity, total classification accuracy) on the test sets of the classifiers are presented in Table 6 (Ilbay K et al., 2010), in order to show performance of the classifiers used for classification of the CTS.

All possible sensitivity/specificity pairs for a particular test can be graphed by receiver operating characteristic (ROC) curves. Therefore, the performance of a test can be evaluated by plotting a ROC curve for the test and ROC curves were used to describe the performances of the SVMs. Sensitivity rises rapidly and 1-specificity hardly increases at all until sensitivity becomes high for a good test.

Classifiers	Desired Result	Output Result			
		Normal	Right CTS	Left CTS	Bilateral CTS
RNN	Normal	77	0	0	1
	Right CTS	2	28	0	2
	Left CTS	1	2	22	2
	Bilateral CTS	1	0	2	110
MLPNN	Normal	71	0	0	3
	Right CTS	5	26	1	4
	Left CTS	3	3	21	5
	Bilateral CTS	2	1	2	103

Table 5. Confusion matrix (Ilbay K et al., 2010)

Classifiers	Classification Accuracies (%)				
	Specificity	Sensitivity (Right CTS)	Sensitivity (Left CTS)	Sensitivity (Bilateral CTS)	Total classification accuracy
RNN	95.06	93.33	91.67	95.65	94.80
MLPNN	87.65	86.67	87.50	89.57	88.40

Table 6. The values of the statistical parameters (Ilbay K et al., 2010)

ROC curves which are shown in Figure 4 (Ilbay K et al., 2010) demonstrate the performances of the classifiers on the test files. From the classification results presented in Table 6 and Figure 4 (classification accuracies and ROC curves), one can see that the RNN trained on the features produce considerably high performance than that of the MLPNN.

6. Conclusions

The clinical symptoms and nerve conduction studies for the diagnosis of CTS are explained. The RNNs were used for automated diagnosis of CTS. The performance of the RNNs on the diagnosis of CTS (normal, right CTS, left CTS, bilateral CTS) was investigated. The accuracy of RNNs trained on the features of CTS (right median motor latency, left median motor latency, right median sensory latency, left median sensory latency) was analyzed. The classification accuracies and ROC curves of the classifiers were presented, in order to evaluate the used classifiers. The classification results and the values of statistical parameters indicated that the RNN had considerable success in discriminating the CTS (total classification accuracy was 94.80%). In the further studies, different neural network architectures and training algorithms can be used for obtaining more efficient results.

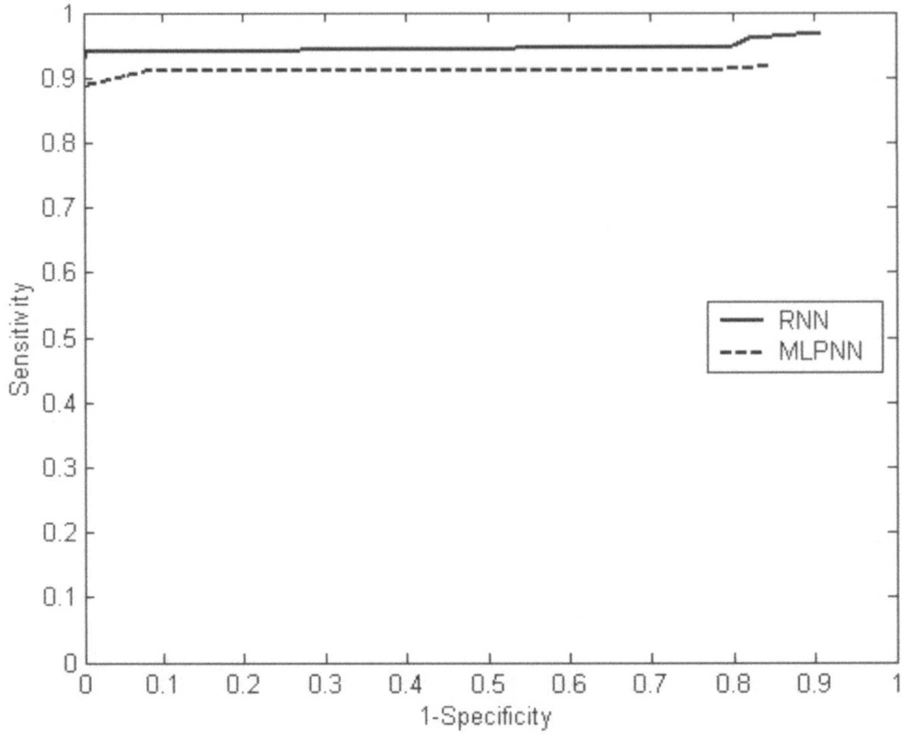

Fig. 4. ROC curves (Ilbay K et al., 2010)

7. References

Aroori, S. & Spence, R.A.J. (2008). Carpal tunnel syndrome. *The Ulster Medical Journal.* Vol. 77, No.1, 6-17, ISSN: 0041-6193.

Basheer, I.A., Hajmeer, M. (2000). Artificial neural networks: fundamentals, computing, design, and application, Journal of Microbiological Methods, 43(1), 3-31.

Battiti, R. (1992). First- and second-order methods for learning: between steepest descent and Newton's method, Neural Computation, 4, 141-166.

Bland, J.D. (2005). Carpal tunnel syndrome. *Current Opinion in Neurology,* Vol.18, No.5, 581-585, ISSN:1350-7540.

Budak, F.; Yenigun, N.; Ozbek, A.; Orhan, S. & Komsuoglu, S. (2001). Carpal tunnel syndrome in carpet weavers. *Electromyography and Clinical Neurophysiology.* Vol. 41, No.1, 29-32, ISSN: 0301-150X.

Chaudhuri, B.B., Bhattacharya, U. (2000). Efficient training and improved performance of multilayer perceptron in pattern classification, Neurocomputing, 34, 11-27.

Cornblath, D.R. & Chaudhry, V. (2001). Electrodiagnostic Evaluation of the Peripheral Neuropathy Patient. In:Mendell, J.R.; Kissel, J.T. & Cornblath D.R., Editors, *Diagnosis and Management of Peripheral Nerve Disorders,* 30-37, Oxford University Press, ISBN: 978-0195133011, USA.

Elman, J.L. (1990). Finding structure in time, Cognitive Science 14(2), 179-211.

Fleckenstein, J.L. & Wolfe, G.I. (2002). MRI vs EMG: Which has the upper hand in carpal tunnel syndrome? *Neurology*. Vol. 58, No. 11, 1583-1584, ISSN: 0028-3878.

Haase, J. (2007). Carpal tunnel syndrome-a comprehensive review. *Advances and Technical Standards in Neurosurgery*. Vol. 32, 175-249, ISSN: 0095-4829.

Hagan, M.T., Menhaj, M.B. (1994). Training feedforward networks with the Marquardt algorithm, IEEE Transactions on Neural Networks, 5(6), 989-993.

Haykin, S. (1994). Neural networks: A Comprehensive Foundation, Macmillan, New York.

Ilbay, K.; Übeyli E.D.; Ilbay, G. & Budak, F. (2010). Recurrent Neural Networks for Diagnosis of Carpal Tunnel Syndrome Using Electrophysiologic Findings. *Journal of Medical Systems* Vol.34, No.4, 643-650, ISSN:0148-5598.

Kamolz, L.P.; Schrögendorfer,K.F; Rab,M.; Girsch,W.; Gruber,H. & Frey,M.(2001). The precision of ultrasound imaging and its relevance for carpal tunnel syndrome. *Surgical and Radiologic Anatomy*. Vol.23, No.2, 117-121, ISSN: 0930-1038.

Kanaan, N. & Sawaya, R.A. (2001). Carpal tunnel syndrome: modern diagnostic and management techniques. *British Journal of General Practice,* Vol.51, No.465, 311-314, ISSN: 0960-1643.

Luchetti, R. (2007). Etiopathogenesis. In: Luchetti, R. & Amadio, P., Editors, *Carpal Tunnel Syndrome,* 21-25, Springer, ISBN: 3-540-22387-8, Germany.

Miller, A.S., Blott, B.H., Hames, T.K. (1992). Review of neural network applications in medical imaging and signal processing, Medical & Biological Engineering & Computing, 30, 449-464.

Pineda, F.J. (1987). Generalization of back-propagation to recurrent neural networks, Physical Review Letters, 59(19), 2229-2232.

Preston, D.C. & Shapiro, B.E. (2005). *Electromyography and Neuromuscular Disorders,* Elsevier Science, ISBN: : 978-0-7506-7492-8, Philadelphia.

Sternbach, G. (1999). The carpal tunnel syndrome. *Journal of Emergency Medicine,* Vol. 17, No.3, 519-523, ISSN:0736-4679.

Sunderland, S. (1976). The nerve lesions of carpal tunnel syndrome. *Journal of Neurology, Neurosurgery, and Psychiatry*. Vol. 39, No. 7, 615-626, ISSN:0022-3050.

Thissen, U., van Brakel, R., Weijer, A.P. de, Melssen, W.J., Buydens, L.M.C. (2003). Using support vector machines for time series prediction, Chemometrics and Intelligent Laboratory Systems, 69, 35-49.

Übeyli, E.D. (2008a). Recurrent neural networks employing Lyapunov exponents for analysis of Doppler ultrasound signals, Expert Systems with Applications, 34(4), 2538-2544.

Übeyli, E.D. (2008b). Recurrent neural networks with composite features for detection of electrocardiographic changes in partial epileptic patients, Computers in Biology and Medicine, 38(3), 401-410.

Übeyli, E.D. (2009a). Analysis of EEG signals by implementing eigenvector methods/recurrent neural networks, Digital Signal Processing, 19(1), 134-143.

Übeyli, E.D. (2009b). Combining recurrent neural networks with eigenvector methods for classification of ECG beats, Digital Signal Processing, 19(2), 320-329.

Übeyli, E.D., Übeyli, M. (2008). Case Studies for Applications of Elman Recurrent Neural Networks, Recurrent Neural Networks, *I-Tech Education and Publishing*, Editors: Xiaolin Hu, P. Balasubramaniam, ISBN 978-953-7619-08-4, Chapter 17, pp.357-376.

von Schroeder, H.P. & Botte, M.J. (1996). Carpal tunnel syndrome. *Hand Clinics,* Vol.12, No.4, 643-655, ISSN: 0749-0712.

4

Modeling of Hysteresis in Human Meridian System with Recurrent Neural Networks

Yonghong Tan, Ruili Dong and Hui Chen
College of Information, Mechanical and Electrical Engineering
Shanghai Normal University
China

1. Introduction

In the theory of the traditional Chinese medicine, it has been found that the acupuncture-points are distributed in the meridian system of the human body. Moreover, meridian system is an independent system which exists in the body parallel with neural systems and blood circulation systems (Tsuei 1998, Trentini et. al. 2005). The experimental results have shown that the meridian system has significant effect on human health (Tsuei, 1998). Based on the recent research results, it was illustrated that the meridian system had an architecture with many channels allowing the electrical signals passed through easily (Zhang et. al. 1999, Yang 1997). That could be used to explain why the acupuncture-therapy would treat some diseases in human body by implementing some stimulating signals on the related acupuncture points. The acupuncture points distributed in the meridian system possesses some distinctive ways for transferring signals and processing information including electrical information (Yang 1997).

Until today, there have been some research results on human meridian system focusing on the analysis of impedance on single acupuncture-point (Yamamoto and Yamamoto 1987, Yang 1997, Zhang et. al. 1999). However, the meridian system is, in fact, a network with several channels. In each channel, there are several acupuncture-points located along a curve. The experimental results demonstrated that there were some relations among those points in each channel. Therefore, the analysis just depending on the impedance of one single acupuncture-point would not reflect the main characteristic of the signal transmission in human meridian system. One of the options is to use an excitation signal to stimulate an acupuncture-point in a channel of the meridian. Then the corresponding response of another acupuncture-point in the same channel is measured. Thus, the signal transmission performance of the measured channel in the meridian can be evaluated. Moreover, the experimental results have demonstrated that the human meridian system is a dynamic system (Zhang et. al. 1999, Yang 1997, Wang et. al. 2009). In this case, the identification of the model to describe the dynamic behavior of the meridian is an efficient way for performance evaluation. Wang et. al. (2009) developed an auto-regressive and moving average model to describe the human meridian system. It fits the response well when the exciting signal with slow frequency and the input amplitude is rather small. However, when the frequency of the exciting input is higher or the amplitude of the exciting signal is larger, it will illustrate some nonlinear behavior. Thus, a nonlinear dynamic model should be considered to describe this system.

This chapter is organized as follows: In the 2nd section of this chapter, a brief description on the scheme of experiments to obtain the response of acupoints in a channel of the human meridian system by stimulating the acupoint in the same channel. Then, in the 3rd section, the analysis of the hysteretic characteristic happened in the response between two acupuncture-points in the same channel is illustrated. In section 4, an expanded input space is constructed to transform the multi-valued mapping of hysteresis to a one-to-one mapping. Then the recurrent neural network is employed to model both dynamics and nonlinearity of the meridian system. As neural network is a non-convex system, it is often stuck in local minima during the training. Therefore, we proposed a dynamic neural network based model with extreme learning machine (ELM) (Huang et. al. 2006 and 2007) to model the dynamic behavior of the human meridian system in section 5. In the scheme, the values of the parameters of the hidden neurons and the weights connecting the hidden neurons with the inputs are specified by random values. The feedback factors connecting the outputs of the hidden nodes with the inputs of the hidden neurons are constrained within the region between zero and one to guarantee the stability of the neural network. However, the weights which interconnect the output of the network and the output of the hidden neurons are determined by least squares (LS) algorithm. In this case, the training of the neural network becomes an optimization for a convex system. Hence, the very good modeling results are derived. The corresponding experimental results are presented in section 6. In the experiment, both traditional ELM neural network and the proposed recurrent version are implemented to model the hysteresis in meridian system. The model validation results have shown that the proposed method has led to much better modeling performance.

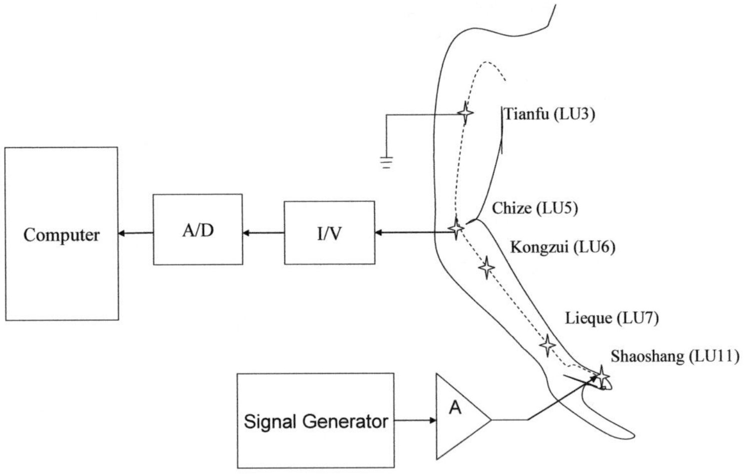

Fig. 1. Experimental Configuration of Measurement of Human Meridian Signal

2. Brief description of the experimental configuration

In this section, a method based on three detecting electrodes is used to measure both stimulation and the corresponding response of the acupuncture-points in meridian systems.

The architecture of the measurement for meridian response is shown in Fig. 1. Based on the theory of Chinese medicine, there are 11 acupoints in the so-called *Hand-Taiyin Lung Channel*. In this experiment, the stimulating acupoint was *Shaoshang (LU 11)*, the acupoint *Tianfu (LU 3)* was connected to ground, and the detecting acupoints were *Chize (LU 5)*, *Kongzui (LU 6)* and *Lieque (LU 7)*, respectively. The stimulation current signals were generated by a signal generator. Then, the signal was amplified by the amplifier A. In this experiment, Acupoint *Shaoshang(LU11)* was excited by the stimulation signals through a stimulating electrode. Then, the detecting electrode was used to measure the corresponding response of acupoint *Chize(LU5)* or the other acupoints in the same channel. The measured output was transferred through a current/ voltage conversion circuit then sampled by an analog /digital (A/D) convertor. The sampled signals were sent to the computer for further processing.

There were 6 healthy volunteers accepted the test. Before the test, the volunteers were relaxed to avoid the strenuous disturbance.

3. The Response of the acupoint of the human meridian

What the behavior of human meridian system to excitations would be? In this section, the experimental results will be presented to show the responses of the acupoint of the human meridian system to the excitation signals.

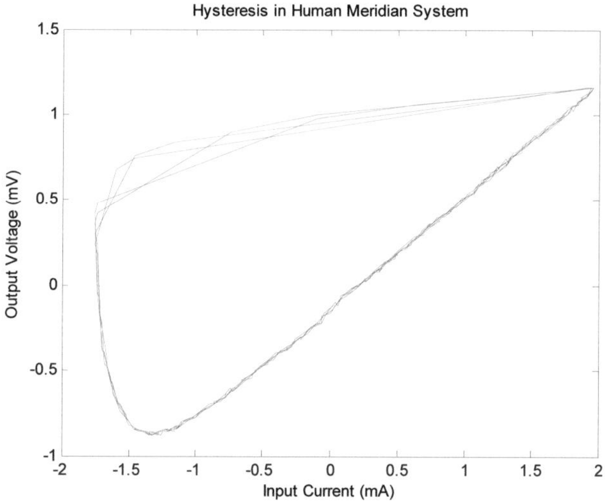

Fig. 2. The plot of the output of acupoint *LU5* against the sawtooth input

In the experiments, we use a sawtooth waveform sequence to excite the meridian. A very interesting thing is that hysteresis phenomenon occurs in the human meridian systems. Fig. 2 shows the plot of the output of acupoint *LU5* against the sawtooth waveform input. Obviously, the hysteresis presents asymmetric dynamic behavior in the response of the acupoint to the sawtooth waveform signal. During the upward segment, the output of the acupoint *LU5* is almost a straight line. However, we can see the slower dynamics in the downward segment of the response. The asymmetric dynamic behavior implies the meridian is a nonlinear dynamic system.

Moreover, From Fig. 2, we note that the hysteretic phenomenon happened in human meridian systems involved with the following characteristics：

1. non-smoothness;
2. multi-valued mapping;
3. asymmetry; and
4. slow time-varying.

Therefore, it is a dynamic system with rather complex characteristics. It is a real challenge to build a model to describe the meridian system with such comprehensive phenomena based on the conventional identification technique because the conventional identification methods can only be useful for the systems with smooth and one-to-one mapping. Hence, it is a challenge to construct a model of hysteresis.

4. Modelling of hysteresis via Neural Networks

Until today, there have been some modeling methods for hysteresis, e.g. Preisach model (Hu 2003) and Prandtl-Ishlinskii (PI) model (Macki et. al. 1993). Those methods used simple backlash operators as the basis functions for modeling. Therefore, lots of operators should be employed in order to obtain accurate models. Although there have been some modified Preisach model (Hu 2003, Ge and Jouaneh 1995 Ang et. al. 2003) and modified PI model (Dong and Tan 2010) proposed to describe the hysteresis systems, the structures of those modified schemes are still very complex. In order to simplify the architecture of the model to describe the behavior of hysteresis, Li and Tan (2004) as well as Zhao and Tan (2006) developed the so-called expanded input space based hysteretic models. In the expanded input space, a hysteretic operator which extracted the main movement feature of the hysteresis was introduced as one of the coordinates. Thus, the multi-valued mapping of hysteresis could be transformed to a one-to-one mapping between the inputs and output. Then, the feedforward neural networks were implemented to model the hysteresis based on the constructed expanded input space. However, due to the non-convex characteristics of the feedforward neural networks, one often met the problem that the training was easily stuck in local minima. It would have significant effect on the performance of the obtained neural models.

In this chapter, a modified scheme of the hysteretic operator given by Zhao and Tan (2006) is proposed. The modified hysteretic operator will handle the case of extreme-missing. Thus, a corresponding expanded input space is constructed. Then, the multi-valued mapping between the input and output of the hysteresis is transformed to a one-to-one mapping on this expanded input space. After that, the extreme learning machine (ELM) (Huang et. al. 2006 and 2007) is applied to the modeling of the hysteresis in human meridian systems.

In order to transform the multi-valued mapping of hysteresis to a one-to-one mapping, based on the expanded input space (Li and Tan 2004, Zhao and Tan 2006), which is a two-dimensional plane consisting of the input of hysteresis as well as the output of the hysteretic operator, is constructed. As the hysteretic operator can extract the movement tendency, such as increase, decrease and turning of the hysteresis, on this plane, the output of the hysteresis corresponding to the point in the input plane can be uniquely determined. One of the advantages of the expanded input space is that the one-to-one mapping between the input space and the output of the hysteresis can be constructed. Thus, the techniques for nonlinear modeling can be implemented to model the behavior of hysteresis on the constructed input space. Moreover, another advantage of this modeling method is that the computation of gradients at non-smooth points can be avoided.

Assumption: The considered hysteresis is continuous and forms a closed loop in the input-output diagram when the input cycles between two extrema.

Then, we define the hysteresis operator $f(x)$ as:

$$f(x) = (1 - e^{|x - x_p|})(x - x_p) + f(x_p) \tag{1}$$

where x is the current input, $f(x)$ is the current output, x_p is the dominant extremum adjacent to the current input x. $f(x_p)$ is the output of the operator when the input is x_p.

The properties of the hysteretic operator are as follows:

1. Let $x(t) \in C(R^+)$, where $R^+ = \{t \mid t \geq 0\}$ and $C(R^+)$ is the sets of continuous functions on R^+. For the different time instance t_1 and t_2, it results in $t_1 \neq t_2$ but $x(t_1) = x(t_2)$, where $x(t_1)$ and $x(t_2)$ are not the extrema. Then it leads to $f[x(t_1)] \neq f[x(t_2)]$.
2. If there exist two time instance t_1 and t_2, also $t_1 \neq t_2$, such that $f[x(t_1)] - f[x(t_2)] \to 0$, then $x(t_1) - x(t_2) \to 0$.

Note that the hysteretic operator used by Zhao and Tan (2006) might encounter the problem that the output extreme of the hysteretic operator might be missed when the input just passes through the extreme. Therefore, in this section, a modified scheme of the hysteresis operator will be proposed.

Note that some extrema might be missed when the input just passed through its extrma. For example, suppose t_1 and t_2 ($t_1 < t_2$) to be two time instances, in this case, if the corresponding values of the input at those two time instances are equal to each other, but the output of the hysteretic operator corresponding to one of the input value is in the increase zone while the output of the operator with respect to another input value is in the decrease zone. The extrema between those two output values of the hysteresis is obviously missed. To handle this problem, we have

Lemma 1: For the formula to describe the hysteresis operator shown in Eq. (1), if $x(t_1) = x(t_2)$, $f[x(t_1)] \neq f[x(t_2)]$, where t_1 and t_2 are the adjacent time instances and $t_1 < t_2$, the extrema located in the segment between points $(x(t_1), f(x(t_1)))$ and $(x(t_2), f(x(t_2)))$ can not be obtained within the time period $[t_1, t_2]$. However, it can be estimated by $(x_m, lm(t_2, t_1))$, where

$$x_m = x(t_2) + 0.5(x(t_2) - x(t_1)),$$

and

$$lm(t_2, t_1) = \begin{cases} (1 - e^{-x_m + x_p})(x_m - x_p) + f(x_p), & x(t_2) > x(t_1) \\ (1 - e^{x_m - x_p})(x_m - x_p) + f(x_p), & x(t_2) < x(t_1) \end{cases}.$$

Proof: Suppose x_m is the local maximum of the input, whilst $x(t_1)$ and $x(t_2)$ are located in the increase and decrease zones, respectively.

Hence, the derivatives of $f(x(t))$ with respect to $x(t)$ at t_2 and t_1 are

$$\dot{f}(x(t_2)) = e^{-x(t_2) + x_p} \tag{2}$$

and

$$\dot{f}(x(t_1)) = e^{-x(t_1)+x_p}, \tag{3}$$

respectively.

Based on the assumption given by Zhao and Tan (2006), $(x_p, f(x_p))$ is a local minimum, and $(x(t_1), f(x(t_1)))$ is a point adjacent to the local maximum point $(x_m, lm(t_2,t_1))$. Hence, $\dot{f}(x(t_2)) \approx \dot{f}(x(t_1))$ due to the properties of exponential function. That is to say, the three points, i.e. $(x(t_1), f(x(t_1)))$, $(x(t_2), f(x(t_2)))$ and $(x_m, lm(t_2,t_1))$ can be considered to be approximately located in a straight line. Moreover, $(x_m, lm(t_2,t_1))$ is the point between $(x(t_1), f(x(t_1)))$ and $(x(t_2), f(x(t_2)))$, where t_1 and t_2 are the adjacent time instances. Define $L(t_2,t_1)$ represents the line connecting $(x(t_1), f(x(t_1)))$ with $(x(t_2), f(x(t_2)))$. So the extremum point in the space can be approximated to be the mean values of the projections of $L(t_2,t_1)$ on each coordinates in the plane. In other words, the mean value of the projection on the input coordinate is estimated by

$$x_m = x(t_2) + 0.5(x(t_2) - x(t_1)), \tag{4}$$

and the mean value of the projection on the coordinate of the output of the hysteretic operator is estimated by

$$lm(t_2,t_1) = (1 - e^{-x_m+x_p})(x_m - x_p) + f(x_p). \tag{5}$$

Similarly, if $(x_m, lm(t_2,t_1))$ is a local minimum, $lm(t_2,t_1)$ can be described by

$$lm(t_2,t_1) = (1 - e^{x_m-x_p})(x_m - x_p) + f(x_p). \tag{6}$$

Hence, combining Eqs.(4), (5) and (6) leads to

$$lm(t_2,t_1) = \begin{cases} (1 - e^{-x_m+x_p})(x_m - x_p) + f(x_p), & x(t_2) > x(t_1) \\ (1 - e^{x_m-x_p})(x_m - x_p) + f(x_p), & x(t_2) < x(t_1) \end{cases}. \tag{7}$$

Therefore, based on the above mentioned Lemma and the following Lemmas given by Zhao and Tan (2006), i.e.

Lemma 2: Let $x(t) \in C(R^+)$, where $R^+ = \{t \mid t \geq 0\}$ and $C(R^+)$ are the sets of continuous functions on R^+. If there exist two time instants t_1, t_2 and $t_1 \neq t_2$, such that $x(t_1) = x(t_2)$, $x(t_1)$ and $x(t_2)$ are not the extrema, then $f\left[x(t_1)\right] \neq f\left[x(t_2)\right]$.

The details of the proofs can be referred to Appendix A.

Lemma 3: If there exist two time instants t_1, t_2 and $t_1 \neq t_2$, such that $f[x(t_1)] - f[x(t_2)] \to 0$, then $x(t_1) - x(t_2) \to 0$.

The corresponding proof of lemma 3 can be referred to Appendix B.

Then, we have the following theorem, i.e.

Theorem: For any hysteresis satisfying Assumption, there exists a continuous one-to-one mapping *Γ*: *R*₂→*R*, such that $F[x(t)] = \Gamma[x(t), f(x(t))]$.

The detail of the proof can be referred to Appendix C.
It can also been proved that the obtained expanded input space is a compact set (Zhao and Tan 2006) Hence, the mapping between the output and the input of the hysteresis on this expanded input space is a one-to-one mapping. Thus, the neural networks such as multilayer feedforward neural network can be implemented to model the performance of hysteresis on this input space.

5. Recurrent ELM NN based model of hysteresis in human meridian systems

Note the non-convex characteristic is one of the main drawbacks of the feedforward neural networks. It is often stuck in some local minima during the training procedure. Moreover, the slow convergence in training is kept it from the application in real-time cases. Huang et. al. (2006 and 2007) have proposed an efficient algorithm called as extreme learning machine (ELM) with the randomly specified input weights of the single hidden layered and the output weights of the network to be determined by using the least squares algorithm. ELM has achieved very good performance in generalization and much faster learning speed. The brief description of this neural network is presented as follows：

For N samples $\{(x_k, t_k)\}_{k=1}^{N}$, where $\mathbf{x}_k = [x_{k1}, x_{k2}, \cdots, x_{kn}]$ is the kth input vector and $\mathbf{t}_k = [t_{k1}, t_{k2}, \cdots, t_{kn}]$ is the kth target vector, a single layer feedforward network (SLFN) with $\tilde{N}$ hidden neurons and activation function $g(x)$, i.e.

$$\sum_{i=1}^{\tilde{N}} \boldsymbol{\beta}_i g(\mathbf{w}_i \cdot \mathbf{x}_k + b_i) = \mathbf{o}_k, k = 1, \cdots, N\ , \tag{8}$$

where $\mathbf{w}_i = [w_{i1}, w_{i2}, \cdots, w_{in}]^T$ is the weight vector connecting the ith hidden neuron and the input neurons, $\boldsymbol{\beta}_i = [\beta_{i1}, \beta_{i2}, \cdots, \beta_{im}]^T$ is the weight vector connecting the ith hidden neuron and the output neurons, $\mathbf{o}_k = [o_{k1}, o_{k2}, \cdots, o_{km}]^T$ is the output vector of the SLFN, and b_i is the threshold of the ith hidden neuron. Moreover, $\mathbf{w}_i \cdot \mathbf{x}_k$ denotes the inner product of $\mathbf{w}_i$ and $\mathbf{x}_k$. Hence, these N equations can be written compactly as:

$$\mathbf{H}\boldsymbol{\beta} = \mathbf{O}\ , \tag{9}$$

where $\mathbf{H}$ is called the hidden layer output matrix, i.e.

$$\mathbf{H} = \begin{bmatrix} g(\mathbf{w}_1 \cdot \mathbf{x}_1 + b_1) & \cdots & g(\mathbf{w}_{\tilde{N}} \cdot \mathbf{x}_1 + b_{\tilde{N}}) \\ \vdots & \cdots & \vdots \\ g(\mathbf{w}_1 \cdot \mathbf{x}_N + b_1) & \cdots & g(\mathbf{w}_{\tilde{N}} \cdot \mathbf{x}_N + b_{\tilde{N}}) \end{bmatrix}_{N \times \tilde{N}}, \tag{10}$$

$$\boldsymbol{\beta} = \begin{bmatrix} \boldsymbol{\beta}_1^T \\ \vdots \\ \boldsymbol{\beta}_{\tilde{N}}^T \end{bmatrix}_{\tilde{N} \times m} \tag{11}$$

and

$$\mathbf{O} = \begin{bmatrix} \mathbf{o}_1^T \\ \vdots \\ \mathbf{o}_N^T \end{bmatrix}_{N\times m} . \tag{12}$$

By randomly assigning and fixing the input weights $\mathbf{w}_i$ and biases b_i, only leaving output weights $\boldsymbol{\beta}_i$ to be adjusted according to the objective function:

$$\min_{\boldsymbol{\beta}} \|\mathbf{H}\boldsymbol{\beta} - \mathbf{T}\|^2 . \tag{13}$$

Based on theorem shown in section 4, the behavior of the hysteresis inherent in meridian system can be modeled by the ELM method on the obtained expanded input space. Therefore, the corresponding ELM based model for hysteresis is shown as follows:

$$\begin{aligned} \boldsymbol{\Gamma}[x, f(x)] &= \mathbf{H}[x, f(x)]\boldsymbol{\beta} + \boldsymbol{\varepsilon} \\ &= \begin{bmatrix} g(\mathbf{w}_1 \cdot [\mathbf{x}_1, f(\mathbf{x}_1)] + b_1) & \cdots & g(\mathbf{w}_{\tilde{N}} \cdot [\mathbf{x}_1, f(\mathbf{x}_1)] + b_{\tilde{N}}) \\ \vdots & \cdots & \vdots \\ g(\mathbf{w}_1 \cdot [\mathbf{x}_N, f(\mathbf{x}_N)] + b_1) & \cdots & g(\mathbf{w}_{\tilde{N}} \cdot [\mathbf{x}_N, f(\mathbf{x}_N)] + b_{\tilde{N}}) \end{bmatrix} \begin{bmatrix} \boldsymbol{\beta}_1^T \\ \vdots \\ \boldsymbol{\beta}_{\tilde{N}}^T \end{bmatrix} + \boldsymbol{\varepsilon} , \end{aligned} \tag{14}$$

where $\boldsymbol{\varepsilon}$ is the modeling error vector, for any given $\varepsilon_N > 0$, $\|\boldsymbol{\varepsilon}\| \le \varepsilon_N$.
By observing the response of the acupoints of human meridian systems, we can see that the dynamics in involved in the hysteresis. In order to describe the dynamic phenomenon of the hysteresis in meridian system, an internal feedback connection is introduced for each hidden neuron in the ELM neural network. Thus, we obtain a so-called recurrent ELM neural network on the constructed expanded input space for hysteresis inherent in human meridian. For a single input-single output network, the corresponding architecture is shown in Fig. 3. Obviously, we have

$$\boldsymbol{\Gamma}[x(t), f(x(t))] = \mathbf{H}[\mathbf{x}(t), f(\mathbf{x}(t)), \mathbf{z}(t-1)]\boldsymbol{\beta} + \boldsymbol{\varepsilon} \tag{15}$$

where

$$\boldsymbol{\beta} = \begin{bmatrix} \boldsymbol{\beta}_1^T \\ \vdots \\ \boldsymbol{\beta}_{\tilde{N}}^T \end{bmatrix}$$

and

$$\mathbf{H}[\mathbf{x}(t), f(\mathbf{x}(t)), \mathbf{z}(t-1)] = \begin{bmatrix} g(\mathbf{w}_1 \cdot [\mathbf{x}_1(t), f(\mathbf{x}_1(t))] + \alpha_1 z_1(t-1)) & \cdots & g(\mathbf{w}_{\tilde{N}} \cdot [\mathbf{x}_1(t), f(\mathbf{x}_1(t))] + \alpha_{\tilde{N}} z_{\tilde{N}}(t-1)) \\ \vdots & \cdots & \vdots \\ g(\mathbf{w}_1 \cdot [\mathbf{x}_N(t), f(\mathbf{x}_N(t))] + +\alpha_1 z_1(t-1)) & \cdots & g(\mathbf{w}_{\tilde{N}} \cdot [\mathbf{x}_N(t), f(\mathbf{x}_N(t))] + \alpha_{\tilde{N}} z_{\tilde{N}}(t-1)) \end{bmatrix}$$

where α_i is the feedback factor with the value randomly assigned within (0,1) to guarantee the stability of the model and

$$z_i(t) = g(\mathbf{w}_i \cdot [\mathbf{x}_j(t), f(\mathbf{x}_j(t))] + \alpha_i z_i(t-1)),\ i = 1,...,N;\ j = 1,...,\tilde{N}\,.$$

For the assigned matrix $\mathbf{H}[.]$, its **QR** decomposition is a matrix of the form

$$\mathbf{H} = \mathbf{QR} \tag{16}$$

where **R** is an upper triangular matrix and **Q** is an orthogonal matrix, i.e., one satisfying

$$\mathbf{Q}^{\mathrm{T}}\mathbf{Q} = \mathbf{I} \tag{17}$$

where **I** is the identity matrix. This matrix decomposition can be used to simplify the computation to determine the solution $\boldsymbol{\beta}$, i.e.

$$\hat{\boldsymbol{\beta}} = (\mathbf{R}^{\mathrm{T}}\mathbf{R})^{-1}\mathbf{R}^{\mathrm{T}}\mathbf{Q}^{\mathrm{T}}\boldsymbol{\Gamma}\,. \tag{18}$$

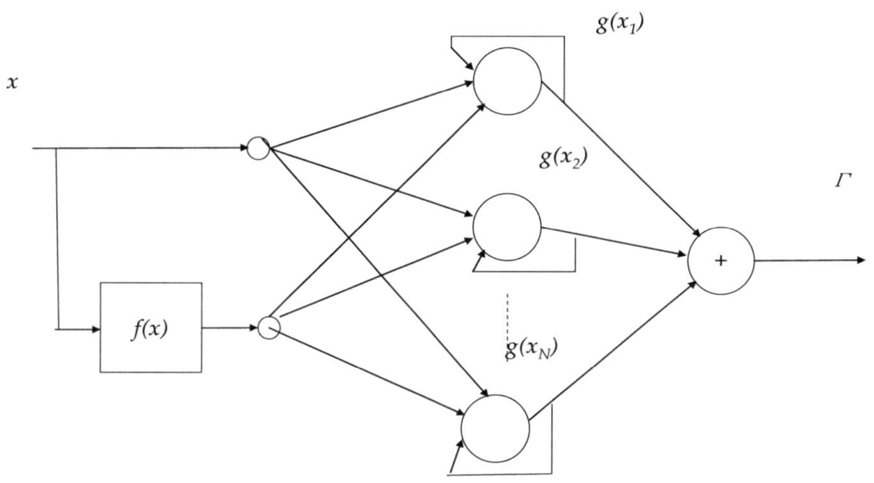

Fig. 3. The structure of recurrent ELM neural network

6. Experimental results

Based on the experimental setup shown in section 2, the experiment to measure the responses of acupoints was implemented. The semi-exponential signal was used to excite the meridian system. Both ELM neural network and recurrent ELM neural network were applied to modelling of the hysteresis happened in the meridian.

Firstly, we applied the ELM neural network with 30 hidden neurons to the modelling procedure of hysteresis. The QR decomposed least square algorithm was utilized to determine the weights of the neural model.

Fig. 4 shows the model validation result of the ELM neural network based model. It can be seen that the model failed to describe the hysteresis occurred in the meridian. On the other hand, we also applied the proposed recurrent ELM neural network on the constructed expanded input space. In the experiment, only 20 hidden neurons were involved in the network. The training algorithm to specify the weights of the model was the same as that in the training of ELM neural model. Fig. 5 illustrates the corresponding performance of model validation. Obviously, the proposed modelling method has achieved satisfactory result. Moreover, the proposed method has used less number of hidden neurons than that of the conventional ELM neural model. Thus, a much simpler model structure has been obtained.

7. Conclusion

A modeling method for hysteresis in human meridian systems is presented. In this modeling scheme, a modified hysteretic operator is proposed to construct an expanded input space to transform the multi-valued mapping of hysteresis into a one-to-one mapping. On the constructed expanded input space, the ELM neural network is employed to model the hysteresis inherent in human meridian systems. As the hysteresis in meridian system is an asymmetric and dynamic system, a recurrent ELM neural network is developed. In the proposed recurrent ELM neural network, the output state of each hidden neuron is fed back to its own input to describe the dynamic behavior of the hysteresis. The training of the recurrent ELM neural network is rather simple. A least square algorithm based on QR decomposition is implemented. The experimental results have shown that the proposed recurrent ELM neural model based model obtained much better modeling performance and simpler model structure.

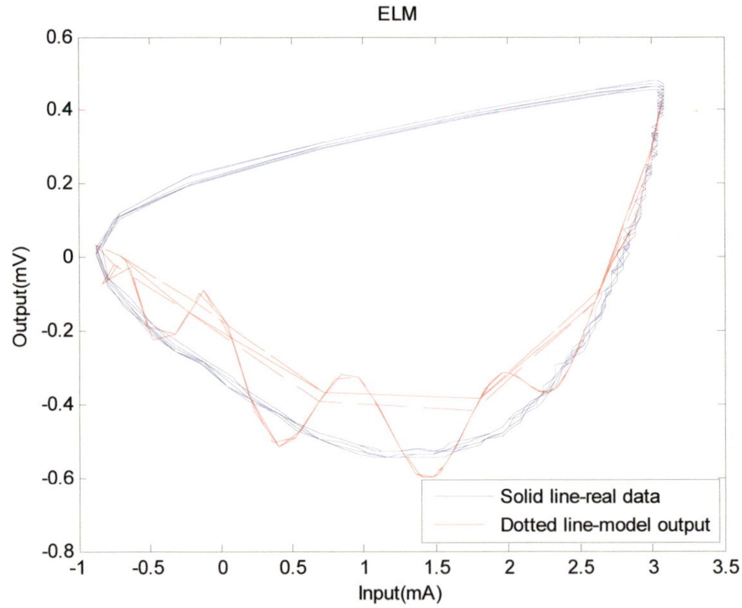

Fig. 4. Model validation of ELM neural network

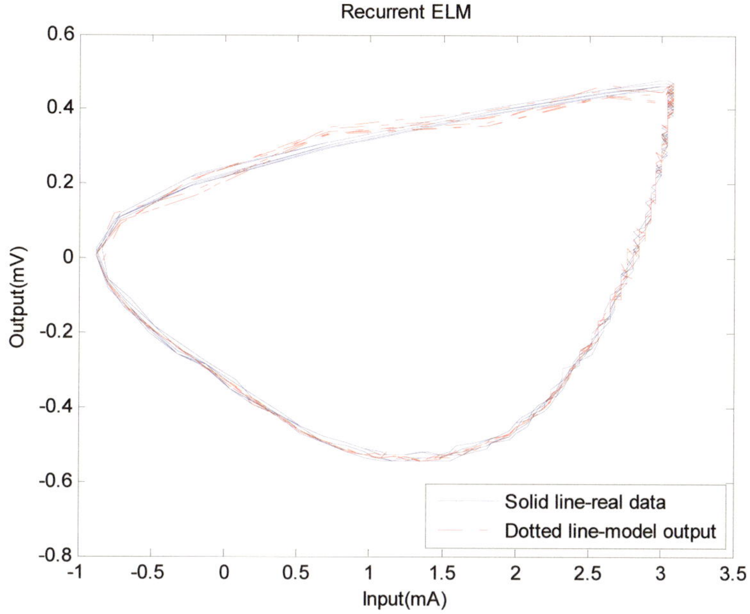

Fig. 5. Model validation of recurrent ELM neural network

8. Appendix A

The proof of lemma 2 is as follows (Zhao and Tan 2006):
Considering the segment $x(t)$ decreases monotonically, (1) becomes

$$f_{de}(x) = (1 - e^{x - x_p})(x - x_p) + f(x_p) \qquad \dot{x}(t) < 0$$

where $f_{de}(x)$ is decreasing segment of the function, x_p is the maximum extremum of the input. Whilst

$$f_{in}(x) = [1 - e^{-(x - x_p)}](x - x_p) + f(x_p) \qquad \dot{x}(t) > 0$$

denotes the increasing segment of the function. In this case, x_p is the minimum extremum of the input. Since

$$\frac{df_{in}(x)}{dx} = e^{-(x - x_p)} \cdot (x - x_p) + [1 - e^{-(x - x_p)}]$$

$$= 1 - \frac{1 - (x - x_p)}{e^{x - x_p}} > 1 - \frac{1}{e^{x - x_p}} > 0 .$$

Therefore, $f_{in}(x)$ is monotonic. Similarly one can obtain that $f_{de}(x)$ is also monotonic.

9. Appendix B

The following is the proof of lemma 3 (Zhao and Tan 2006).
Consider the case of $\dot{x}(t) > 0$ that means in increase segment of the hysteresis. Assume that the segment *x(t)* increases monotonically. From the proof of Lemma 1, it follows that

$$f_{in}(x) = [1 - e^{-(x-x_p)}](x - x_p) + f(x_p)$$

is monotonic as $x(t_1) - x(t_2) \to 0$. Thus, it yields

$$f_{in}\left[x(t_1)\right] - f_{in}\left[x(t_2)\right] \to 0 .$$

In terms of the property of continuity of the inverse function, it yields

$$f_{in}\left[x(t_1)\right] - f_{in}\left[x(t_2)\right] \to 0 ,$$

thus $x(t_1) - x(t_2) \to 0$. Similarily, when

$$f_{de}\left[x(t_1)\right] - f_{de}\left[x(t_2)\right] \to 0 \text{, it results in}$$

$$x(t_1) - x(t_2) \to 0 .$$

10. Appendix C

Firstly, it is proved that Γ is a one-to-one mapping.
Case 1: Assume that *x*(*t*) is not the extremum. In terms of lemma1, if there exist two different time instances t_1 and t_2, then

$$\left(x(t_1), f\left[x(t_1)\right]\right) \neq \left(x(t_2), f\left[x(t_2)\right]\right) .$$

Therefore, the coordinate (*x*(*t*), *f*[*x*(*t*)]) is uniquely corresponding to hysteresis *H*[*x*(*t*)].
Case 2: Suppose that *x*(*t*) is the extremum. In this case, for two different time instances *t*1 and *t*2, there will be

$$\left(x(t_1), f\left[x(t_1)\right]\right) = \left(x(t_2), f\left[x(t_2)\right]\right) .$$

According to the property of the Preisach-type hysteresis, $H[x(t_1)] = H[x(t_2)]$. Then the coordinate (*x*(*t*), *f*[*x*(*t*)]) will be uniquely corresponding to hysteresis *H*[*x*(*t*)].
Combining the above-mentioned two situations, it is obtained that Γ is a one-to-one mapping. Next, it will be verified that Γ is a continuous mapping.
According to [11],

$$x(t_1) - x(t_2) \to 0 \quad \Rightarrow H[x(t_1)] - H[x(t_2)] \to 0 .$$

Then, considering lemma 3,

$$f\left[x(t_1)\right] - f\left[x(t_2)\right] \to 0 \Rightarrow x(t_1) - x(t_2) \to 0 \Rightarrow H[x(t_1)] - H[x(t_2)] \to 0 .$$

Therefore, it can be concluded that there exists a continuous one-to-one mapping $\Gamma : R^2 \rightarrow R$ such that $H[x(t)] = \Gamma(x(t), f[x(t)])$.

11. Acknowledgment

This research is partially supported by the Leading Academic Discipline Project of Shanghai Normal University (Grant No.: DZL811), the Innovation Program of Shanghai Municipal Education Commission (Grant Nos.:09ZZ141 and 11YZ92), the Advanced Research Grant of Shanghai Normal University (Grant Nos.: DYL201005 and DRL904), the National Science Foundation of China (NSFC Grant No.:60971004), the Natural Science Foundation of Shanghai (Grant No.: 09ZR1423400) and the Science and Technology Commission of Shanghai Municipality (Grant No.: 09220503000 and 10JC1412200).

12. References

R Becker, M. Reichmanis, A. Marino, J. Spadaro. (1976). Electrophysiological correlates of acupuncture points and meridians. *Psychoenergetic Syst,* Vol.1, 105−12.

R. Dong and Y. Tan. (2009). Modeling Hysteresis in Piezoceramic Actuators Using Modified Prandtl- Ishlinskii Model, *Physica B*, Vol.404, No.8-11, 1336-1342

P. Ge and M. Jouaneh. (1995), Modeling Hysteresis in Piezoceramic Actuators, *Precision Engineering*, Vol. 17, 211-221

G. Huang, Q. Zhu, C. Siew. (2006), Extreme Learning Machine: Theory and Application, *Neurocomputing*, Vol.70, 489-501

G. Huang, L. Chen. (2007). Convex Incremental Extreme Learning Machine, Neurocomputing, Vol.70, 3056–3062

H.Hu and R.Ben Mrad. (2003), On the Classical Preisach Model for Hysteresis in Piezoceramic Actuators, *Mechatronics* . Vol. 13, 85-94.

C. Li, Y. Tan. (2004). A Neural Networks Model for Hysteresis Nonlinearity, *Sensors and Actuators A*, Vol. 112, 49–54

J. W. Macki, P. Nistri, P. Zecca. (1993). Mathematical Models for Hysteresis , *SIAM Review,*Vol.35, No.1, 94-123

R. M, Marino AA, Becker RO. (1975). Electrical Correlatesof Acupuncture Points. *IEEE Trans Biomed Eng*, Vol.22, 533−5.

F. J. Trentini, B. Thompson and J. S. Erlichman. (2005). The Antinociceptive Effect of Acupressure in Rats, *The American Journal of Chinese Medicine*, Vol. 33, No.1,143-150

J. J. Tsuei. (1998). A Modern Interpretation of Acupuncture and the Meridian System. *Proc. of the 2nd lntemational Conference on Bioelectromagnetism,* 177 - 182

V. R. Twenty. (1975). Years of Electroacupuncture Diagnosis in Germany. A progress report. *Am J Acupunct, Vol.;*3, 7−17.

Z. Wang, Y. Tan, M. Su. (2009). Modeling of Meridian Channels, *Proceedings of the International Conference on Biomedical Electronics and Devices,* 167-172

Z. Wlodarski. (2005). Alternative Preisach Models, *Physica B*, Vol.367, 273-242

Y.Yamamoto and T. Yamamoto. (1987). Dynamic System for the Measurement of Electrical Skin Impedance. Med. Prog. Tech. Vol.12, 171-183

H.Y. Yang. (1997). The Research and Application of the Dynamic Testing System for Point Skin Resistance, *Journal of Biomedical Engineering,* Vol.16 No.1, 41-50

W. Zhang, R, Xu and Z. Zhu. (1999). The Influence of Acupuncture on the Impedance measured by four electrodes on Meridians. *Acupunct. & Electro-Therap. Res. Int.J.*, Vol. 24, 181-188.

X. Zhao, Y. Tan. (2006). Neural Network Based Identification of Preisach-type Hysteresis in Piezoelectric Actuator Using Hysteretic Operator, *Sensors and Actuators A,* Vol. 126, 306-311

5

Toward an Integrative Dynamic Recurrent Neural Network for Sensorimotor Coordination Dynamics.

Cheron G.[1,2], Duvinage M.[3], Castermans[3], T. Leurs F.[1], Cebolla A.[1], Bengoetxea A.[1], De Saedeleer C.[2], Petieau M.[2], Hoellinger T.[1], Seetharaman K.[1], Draye JP[1]. and Dan B[4].

[1]*Laboratory of Neurophysiology and Movement Biomechanics, Université Libre de Bruxelles, CP 168, 50 Av F Roosevelt, Brussels,*
[2]*Laboratory of Electrophysiology, University of Mons,*
[3]*TCTS lab, University of Mons,*
[4]*Department of Neurology, Hôpital Universitaire des Enfants reine Fabiola, Université Libre de Bruxelles,*
Belgium

1. Introduction

The utilization of dynamic recurrent neural networks (DRNN) for the interpretation of biological signals coming from human brain and body has acquired a significant growth in the field of brain-machine interface. DRNN approaches may offer an ideal tool for the identification of input-output relationships in numerous types of neural-based signals, such as intracellular synaptic potentials, local field potentials, EEG and EMG which integrate multiple sources of activity distributed across large neuronal assemblies. In the field of motor control, the output signals of the DRNN mapping concern movement-related kinematics signals such as position, velocity or acceleration of the different body segments involved. The most direct input signals consist in the electromyographic signals (EMG) recorded over the different superficial muscles implicated in movement generation. It is generally recognized that the non-invasive recording of the EMG envelope signal represents a reasonable reflection of the firing rate of the motoneuronal pools including both central and afferent influences (Cheron and Godaux, 1986). In addition, the combination of the multiple EMG signals may reveal the basic motor coordination dynamics of the gesture (Scholz and Kelso, 1990; Kelso, 1995). A major interest of the EMGs to kinematics mapping by a DRNN is that it may represent a new indirect way for a better understanding of motor organization elaborated by the central nervous system. After the learning phase and whatever the type of movement, the identification performed by the DRNN offers a dynamic memory which is able to recognize the preferential direction of the physiological action of the studied muscles (Cheron et al. 1996, 2003, 2006, 2007). In this chapter, we present the DRNN structure and the training procedure applied in case of noisy biological signals. Different DRNN applications are here reviewed in order to illustrate their usefulness in the field of motor control as diagnostic tools and potential prosthetic controllers.

2. Multiple EMG signals as a final output controller

The behavior of cortical neurons has been well related to movement segmentation, velocity profiles and EMG patterns (Schwartz and Moran, 1999) confirming the hypothesis that the timing of muscle activation is generated by the central neural structures. For instance, the agonist–antagonist organization of the muscles and the reciprocal mode of command are represented by the activity of a subset of cortical neurons correlated inside of cortical maps, with activation of one group of muscles linked to a simultaneous decrease in the activity of the opposing set of muscles (Cheney et al. 1985; Jackson et al. 2003, 2007; Capaday, 2004). The organization of the EMG burst is, in some instances, the peripheral reflection of the central rhythmical activity of the brain during the movement genesis (Bengoetxea et al. 2010). This rhythmical organization could be viewed as resulting from a motor binding process (Sanes and Truccolo, 2003) supported by the synchronization of cortical neurons forming functional assemblies in the premotor and primary motor cortex (Jackson et al. 2003; Hatsopoulos et al. 2003, 2007; Rubino et al. 2006). Moreover, the timing of the antagonist EMG burst is pre-programmed by the cerebellum and our DRNN has been able to learn and reproduce such aspect of motor control (Cheron et al. 2007). This will permit to use the antagonist EMG burst to stop adequately a prosthetic movement. We have also demonstrated that the DRNN is able to reproduce the major parameters of human limb kinematics such as: (1) fast drawing of complex figure by the upper limb (Cheron et al. 1996, Draye et al. 1997), (2) whole-body straightening (Draye et al. 2002), (3) lower limb movement in human locomotion (Cheron et al. 2003; Cheron et al. 2006) and (4) pointing ballistic movement (Cheron et al. 2007). In all of these experimental situations we have found that the attractor states reached through DRNN learning correspond to biologically interpretable solutions (Cheron et al. 2007). It was recently demonstrated that neural network with continuous attractors might symbolically represent context-dependent retrieval of short-term memory from long-term memory in the brain (Tsuboshita and Okamoto, 2007). Indeed, as recurrent neural networks take context and historical information into account they are recognized as universal approximators of dynamical systems (Hornik et al. 1989; Doya, 1993). This means that the DRNN mapping between EMG to kinematics may give rise to a dynamical controller of human movement.

3. The DRNN structure

Our DRNN is governed by the following equations:

$$T_i \frac{\mathrm{d}y_i}{\mathrm{d}t} = -y_i + F(x_i) + I_i \quad (1)$$

where $F(a)$ is the squashing function $F(a) = (1+e^{-a})^{-1}$, y_i is the state or activation level of unit i, I_t is an external input (or bias), and x_i is given by:

$$x_i = \sum_j w_{ij}\, y_j \quad (2)$$

which is the propagation equation of the network (x_i is called the total or effective input of the neuron, W_{ij} is the synaptic weight between units i and j). The time constants T_i will act like a relaxation process. It allows a more complex dynamical behaviour and improves the non-linearity effect of the sigmoid function (Draye et al. 1996, 1997). In order to make the temporal behaviour of the network explicit, an error function is defined as:

$$E = \int_{t_0}^{t_1} q(y(t),t)\, dt \quad (3)$$

where t_0 and t_1 give the time interval during which the correction process occurs. The function $q(y(t), t)$ is the cost function at time t which depends on the vector of the neuron activations y and on time. We then introduce new variables p_i (called adjoint variables) that will be determined by the following system of differential equations:

$$\frac{dp_i}{dt} = \frac{1}{T_i} p_i - e_i - \sum_j \frac{1}{T_i} w_{ij} F'(x_j) p_j \quad (4)$$

with boundary conditions $p_i(t_1)=0$. After the introduction of these new variables, we can derive the learning equations:

$$\frac{\delta E}{\delta w_{ij}} = \frac{1}{T_i} \int_{t_0}^{t_1} y_i F'(x_j) p_j \, dt \quad (5)$$

$$\frac{\delta E}{\delta T_i} = \frac{1}{T_i} \int_{t_0}^{t_1} p_i \frac{dy_i}{dt} \quad (6)$$

The training is supervised, involving learning rule adaptations of synaptic weights and time constant of each unit (for more details, see Draye et al. 1996). This algorithm is called 'backpropagation through time' and tries to minimize the error value defined as the differential area between the experimental and simulated output kinematics signals.

3.1 Improved DRNN training in case of noisy signals

We found that for certain noisy biological signals, the results obtained using the procedure described above were not satisfying. In some cases the convergence to a minimum error value was very slow or the learning process could lead to some bifurcations, as shown in Figure 1. In order to solve those problems, we brought two improvements to the DRNN training procedure: firstly, by using a convergence acceleration technique, and secondly by developing a technique to optimize the DRNN topology (i.e. the number of hidden neurons) to use.

The convergence acceleration technique we used is inspired from Silva and Almeida (1990). In their method, they defined an adaptive learning rate ε_{ij} different for each inter-neuron connection w_{ij}, namely for each synaptic weight and time constant. The acceleration consists in modifying the learning rate depending on the error function gradient sign. If the sign changes after iterating, it indicates that the learning went too far and so that the learning

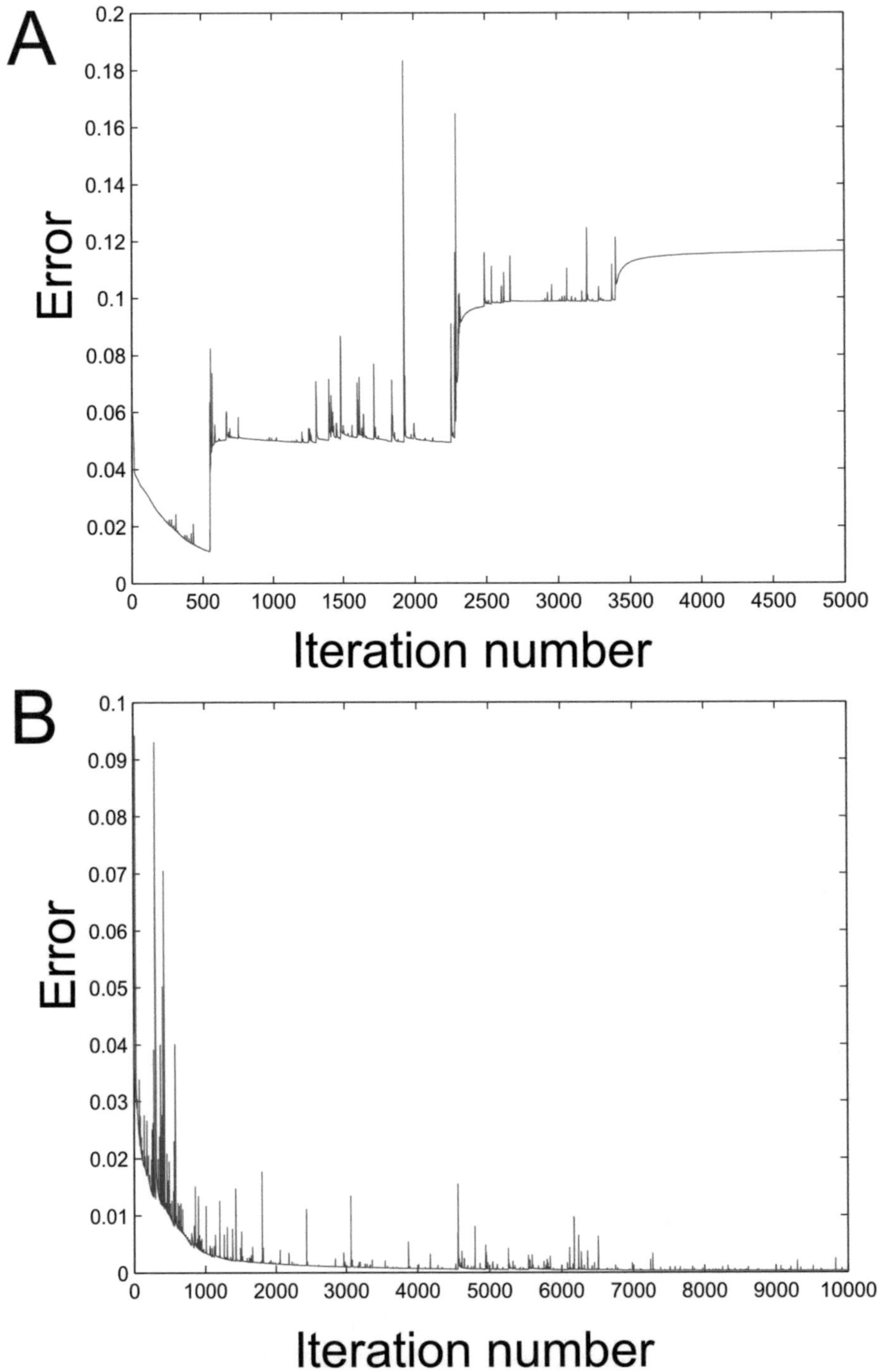

Fig. 1. In A, typical example of a training procedure where the error function increases with the number of iterations before enhancements. In B, same illustration after enhancements.

step is too big. In this case, the learning rate is multiplied by d (by default, d=0.7). If there is no sign change after iterating, it means that the learning rate is too small. It is then multiplied by u (by default, u=1.3) in order to increase the step length and thus accelerate the search for the minimum error value. Formally, the algorithm is the following:

- Small values are chosen for each ε_{ij}
- At the step n, the learning rate is defined as:

  If

$$\frac{\partial E}{\partial w_{ij}}(n) \cdot \frac{\partial E}{\partial w_{ij}}(n-1) \geq 0$$

  Then

$$\varepsilon_{ij}(n) = \varepsilon_{ij}(n\text{-}1) \cdot u$$

  Else

$$\varepsilon_{ij}(n) = \varepsilon_{ij}(n\text{-}1) \cdot d$$

- The connections w_{ij} are incremented:

$$\Delta w_{ij}(n) = -\varepsilon_{ij}(n) \cdot \frac{\partial E}{\partial w_{ij}}(n)$$

We observed that this method effectively accelerates the learning convergence, but can also lead to an abnormal behavior such as a monotonous increase of the error function along the number of learning steps as shown in Figure 1 B. Therefore, a new procedure was developed checking at each learning step if the new learning rate ε_{ij} will not lead to an increase of the error function. In that case, learning rates are halved. For each step n, the mathematic formalism is the following:

If $E(\mathrm{n} + 1) > E(n)$

Then $\varepsilon_{ij}(n) = \varepsilon_{ij}(n)/2$

Thanks to this procedure, the error function exhibits now a much better behavior, as depicted in Figure 2A. Finally, in order to obtain the best results as possible, the parameters that lead to the lowest error are stored along the learning. Thanks to those enhancements, the DRNN has a higher probability to converge in the training phase.

Because the initial values of the parameters are random, a global optimization of the topology is valuable. It consists in training a certain amount of different neural networks with a certain topology and then, the same procedure has to be done again with another topology. Finally, the total amount of DRNNs is tested on another dataset and the best DRNN is chosen based on an error criterion. This criterion can be the sum of training and testing errors, the testing error, or any other combination. Figure 2A and B show respectively the impact of this approach on the link between a noisy and complex signal and the curve of walking kinematics before and after enhancements,

4. DRNN identification of EMG-kinematic relationships during maturation of toddlers' locomotion

The emergence of the very first steps in toddler's locomotion is considered as a milestone in developmental motor physiology because it represents the first basic skill implicating whole body movement in vertical posture upon which goal directed repertoires are built (Cheron

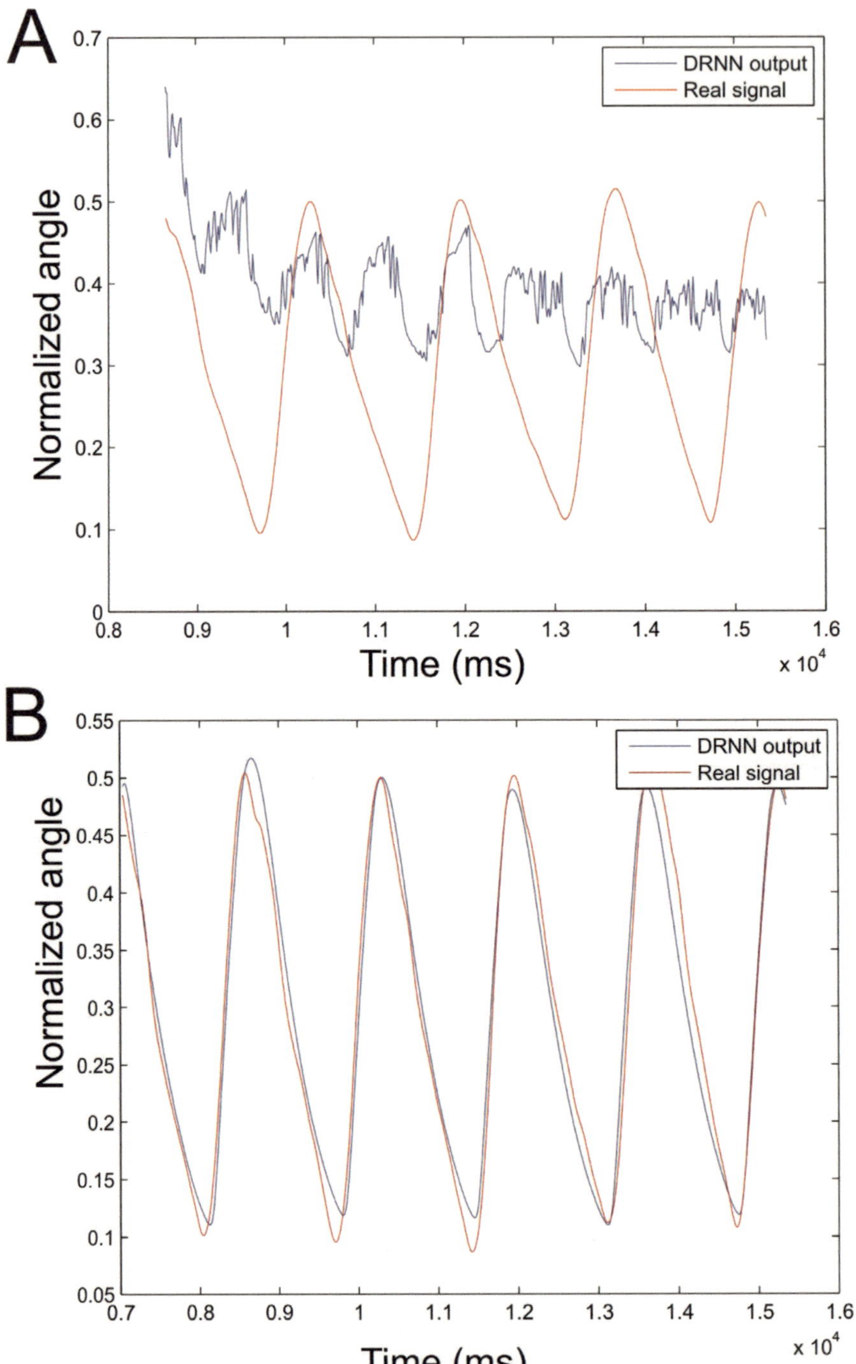

Fig. 2. In A, illustration of a bad result of the DRNN output due to a bifurcation in the training procedure. In B, example of successful results obtained thanks to the acceleration method applied during the training procedure and optimization of the DRNN topology

et al. 2001a,b, 2006; Ivanenko et al. 2004). The generation of the first steps is performed on the basis of highly variable and complex EMG patterns including erratic bursts and co-contractions (Cheron et al. 2006; Okamoto and Goto. 1985, Okamoto and Okamoto, 2001, Okamoto et al. 2003). Such behavioural emergence may be analyzed in the context of neural group selection theory for which final or more stable solutions are selected upon numerous variable and unstable patterns (Edelman, 1987; Sporns and Edelman, 1993; Thelen and Corbetta, 1994; Turvey and Fitzpatrick, 1993). However, classical analytic tools failed to extract such relationships during the first three months of gait maturation. We apply our DRNN methodology previously developed in adult gait (Cheron et al. 2003) here for studying the functional relationships between multiple EMG signals and the elevation angles of the three main segments of the lower limb in toddlers'gait. The first derivative of elevation angles of the thigh, shank and foot were chosen because they represent robust parameters of human locomotion (Borghese et al. 1996; Lacquaniti et al. 1999) including in children (Cheron et al. 2001a).

Despite the recent development of artificial neural networks using multiple EMG time course as input for providing joint torque (Koike and Kawato, 1995; Savelberg and Herzog, 1997), joint angular acceleration (Koike and Kawato, 1994; Draye et al. 2002) or position (Cheron et al. 1996) of the upper limb, this type of mapping has sparsely been used in the field of human locomotion (Sepulveda et al. 1993). Conceptual and technical problems could explain why the neural network approach has been limited in the field of locomotion studies. Walking movement, although seemingly stereotyped, is highly complex as it integrates equilibrium constraints and forward propulsion in a multi-joint system. Therefore separate feedforward neural models could be developed, one for postural control and one for propulsion movement implicating some gating or selecting devices for an appropriate switch between these different networks. Although this type of approach has proved successful for arm movement control (Koike and Kawato, 1994), it is problematic for the control of task with simultaneous postural and movement requirements such as locomotion where distinction between the two modes of control is difficult on the basis of EMG signals. Moreover, in walking the great number of joints and body segments involved pose the problem of choice of the kinematic parameter to be used as the output of the neural mapping. Technically, the majority of neural networks used for EMG-to-kinematics mapping have been of the feedforward type (Sepulveda et al. 1993; Koike and Kawato, 1994). In these networks, information flows from the input neurons to the output neurons without any feedback connections. This excludes context and historical information, which are thought to be crucial in motor control (Kelso, 1995).allowing to take into account time history and re-entrance of information flux into the controller.

As explained above, the DRNN attractor states reached through artificial learning may correspond to biologically interpretable solutions and provide a new way to understand the development of the functional relationship between multiple EMG profiles and the resulting movement. Here, we followed the evolution of these attractor states during the early maturation of gait. As the coupling of neural oscillators between each other and with limb mechanical oscillators is progressively integrated with growing walking experience, we hypothesized that the EMG to kinematics mapping by the DRNN will become an easier task during the maturation of gait. For this, 8 surface EMG and kinematics of the lower limb have been acquired in 9 toddlers, (5 girls and 4 boys) by the motion analysis system ELITE (BTS Italy), during their very first unsupported steps (Fig. 3A). Four toddlers have been acquired on different days preceding and following the onset of independent walking.

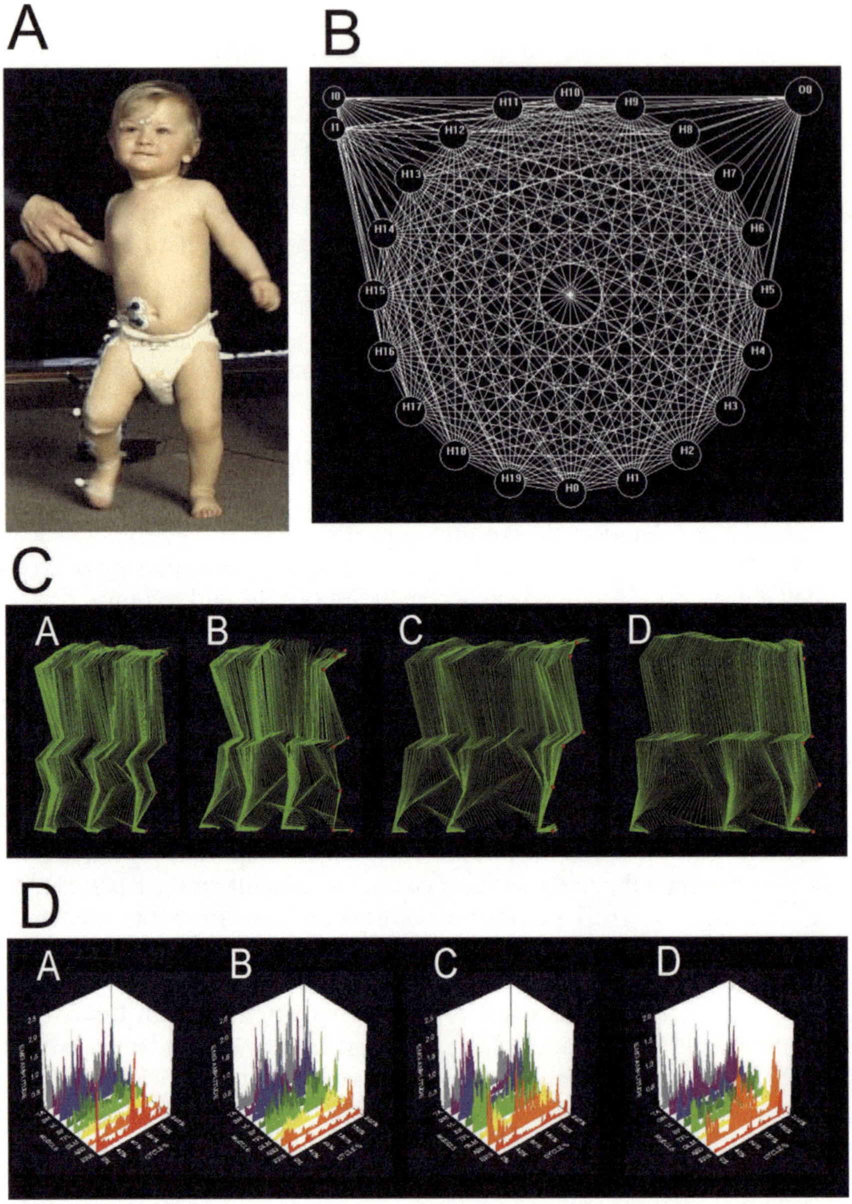

Fig. 3. In A, illustration of one toddler during the acquisition of gait data (A). The kinematics was recorded by the optoelectronic ELITE system (BTS, Italy) and retro-reflective markers fixed on the skin over the following bony landmarks: Fifth Metatarsal Head (5M), Lateral Malleolus (LM), Lateral Condylus (LC), Greater Trochanter (GT), Anterior Iliac Crest (IL), Acromium (AC), Ear (EAR), Nose (NOS). The EMGs were recorded by surface electrodes fixed over the following muscles: Tibialis Anterior (TA), Gastrocnemius Medialis (GM), Vastus Lateralis (VL), Biceps Femoris (BF), Tensor Fascia Lata (TFL), Gluteus Maximus (GLM), Rectus abdominis (ABD) and Erector Spinae (ERS). In B, architecture of the Dynamic Recurrent Neural Network (DRNN), illustrating 20 fully connected Hidden Units

(H0-H19), two Input Units on the left (I0 and I1), and one Output Unit (O0). Note that in this experiment we used 8 Inputs, 3 Outputs and 35 Hidden Units. In C, stick diagrams of one representative toddler on four acquisition days: A: two weeks before the very first unsupported steps. A parent holds one hand of the toddler. B: very first unsupported steps. C: after one week of independent walking experience. D: after 1.5 month of independent walking experience. In D, EMG signals corresponding to the acquisitions of the stick diagrams shown in C. These signals are filtered, rectified and integrated. For each day, at least 3 training sets of two successive walking cycles, starting with "Toe Off" are used in this study.

Informed consent has been given by their parents and the procedures were conformed to the Declaration of Helsinki.

The smoothed and rectified EMG signals of one representative subject are illustrated in Figure 3, C. These signals are sent to all 35 hidden units of the DRNN (Fig. 3B), whose synaptic weights and time constants are adjusted during the supervised learning procedure. In order to quantify the likeness of the simulated output signals with respect to the original one, we calculated a similarity index (SI) using the following equation:

$$SI = \frac{\int f_1(t) f_2(t) dt}{\left[\left(\int f_1(t)^2 dt\right)\left(\int f_2(t)^2 dt\right)\right]^{\frac{1}{2}}}$$

If $f_1(t) = f_2(t)$, then SI = 1.

Then the DRNN output (f_2) is compared to the experimental kinematics' data (f_1) (this correspondence is expressed by SI). If an SI > 0.99 is reached within 10000 iterations, we consider that the training has been successful and its generalization capacities will be tested. The Figure 4A illustrates the artificial learning success rate (ALSR) considered as the ratio of "successful network trainings" (reaching a SI > 0.99 between the acquired kinematics and the simulated ones within 10000 iterations), compared to the total learning trials, for each acquisition day. There is no significant difference in the ALSR (F=2.17; p=0.17) between different days. This means that artificial learning success rates are not significantly related to the degree of early maturation in gait and that the DRNN reach their attractor states whatever the maturation of the input-output signals. The natural variability of the toddler's gait kinematics was assessed by the analysis of the different steps performed during the same day by calculating the same SI used before to qualify the ALSR. In this case, a SI=1 means that there is no variability between the different steps. We found that it is only after 44 days of unsupported walking experience that the pattern is more stabilized. The generalization ability was assessed by the comparison of the kinematics calculated from unlearned EMG of the same acquisition day by a successfully trained DRNN with the kinematics corresponding to this unlearned EMG (Fig. 4C). The recognition index (RI) uses the same formula as the previously calculated SI but in this case the comparison is made between simulation obtained when an unlearned pattern is used as input and the real one. Interestingly, in contrast to the evolution of the SI, the RI presented a regular improvement from the first unsupported steps on to the 44th day (F=7.25; p=0.0003).

We may conclude from these results that while the ALSR is not significantly related to the degree of early maturation in gait, there is a clear improvement of the identification process for the more experienced walking patterns (day 4), which are also more reproducible.

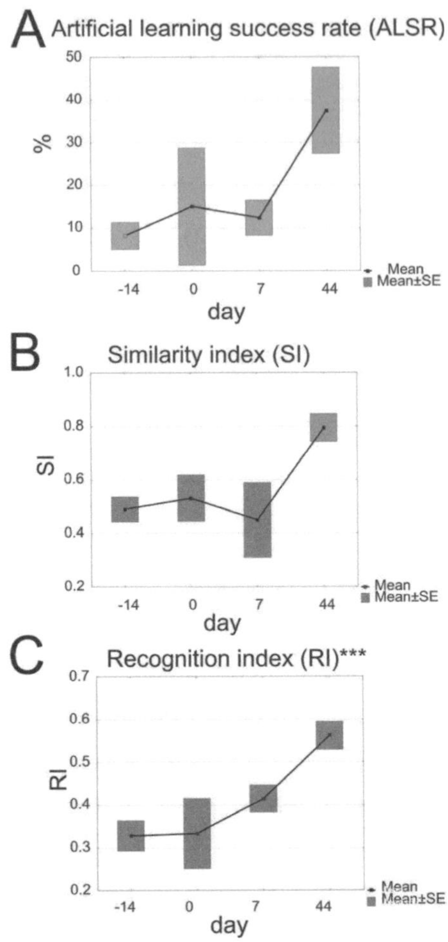

Fig. 4. Histograms of the evolution of the artificial learning success rate (ALSR) (A), the similarity index (SI) (B) and the recognition index (RI).

Correct recognition of unlearned EMG patterns by a trained DRNN is significantly related to the walking experience of the toddler. In this context, the DRNN could be used to follow and quantify the maturation of a toddler's and/or child's gait. The increase in the RI during gait maturation could be interpreted as a better coupling between neural oscillators and limb mechanical oscillators, which could be progressively integrated by toddlers. By this way, the relationship of multiple muscle EMGs and resulting kinematics can slowly be generalized. This fits relatively well with Gibson's concept (1988) suggesting that dynamic patterns emerge through exploration of available solutions before subsequent selection of preferred patterns. (Gibson, 1988). The initial solutions acquired through self-organized principle are often unstable and become more stable with practice. In this initial state, the DRNN can learn but its generalization ability is weak. It is only when behaviours have been practiced sufficiently and when the task and the context are unchanging that stable patterns emerge facilitating the generalization ability of the DRNN. Neurophysiological data are in favour of the existence of a central pattern generator (CPG) involving the spinal and supra spinal levels acting as a dynamic network generating rhythmic leg patterns (Hadders-Algra,

2002; Hadders-Algra et al. 1996). The dynamics of this innate complex progressively emerges through the process of repeated cycles of action and perception (Edelman, 1987; Sporns and Edelman, 1993). Our DRNN approach of EMG to kinematics mapping of toddler's locomotion offers a new investigation tool of such complex processing.

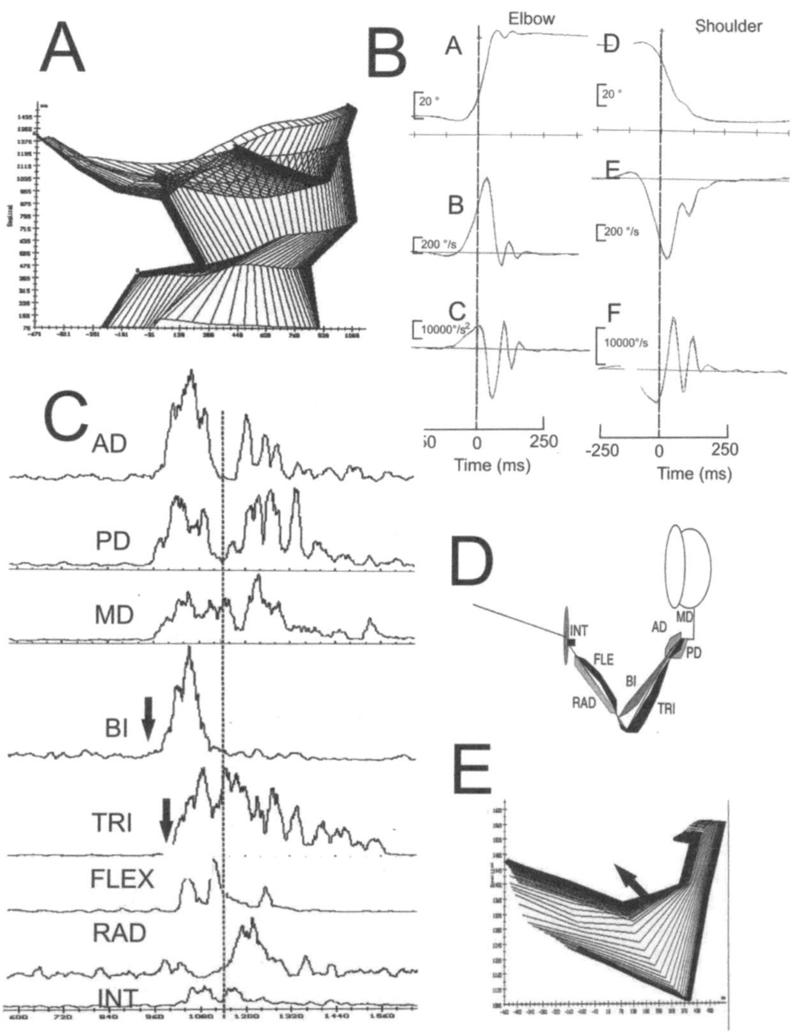

Fig.5. Lunging movement realized by an elite fencer. In A, kinogram of the whole body movement. In B, angular position (A, D), angular velocity (B,E) and angular acceleration of the elbow and the shoulder, respectively. In C, rectified EMG bursts of the anterior deltoïd (AD), posterior deltoïd (PD), medial deltoïd (MD), biceps (BI), triceps (TRI), flexor common (FLEX), radialis (RAD) and interroseus (INT) muscles. In D, simplified sketch of muscles anatomy. In E, kinogram of the upper limb extension movement. The vertical lines correspond to the time of the touch. The black arrows pointed to the onset of the BI and TRI muscles.

5. DRNN approach reveals interaction torque in sport movements

EMG to kinematics mapping was applied to lunging movement performed by elite fencers. This stereotypical movement (Fig. 5A) is a whole body movement, but our mapping was only concerned with the upper limb movement (Fig. 5C) and related muscles (Fig. 5D). The angular acceleration of the shoulder and the elbow (Fig. 5E) were used as output signals and the rectified EMG of 8 superficial muscles (Fig. 5B) as input signals of a DRNN composed in this case of 20 neurons.

The thrusting movement of the upper limb consists of a very rapid extension of the elbow joint (Fig 5B). Logically, this elbow extension should be accomplished by the prime mover action of the triceps (TRI)(Fig. 5C). However, the inspection of the time onset of the EMG burst of the TRI muscles shows that it is not the first event and that the EMG of the biceps muscle (BI) arrives earlier (Fig. 5C and 6C). Quite surprisingly, this muscular strategy only occurred in elite fencers and not in amateur fencers and may be explained by using a peculiar mechanical law implicating the interaction torque between the shoulder and the elbow. Indeed, the EMG recording demonstrated that the BI muscle is the prime mover of the extension. How this can be done?

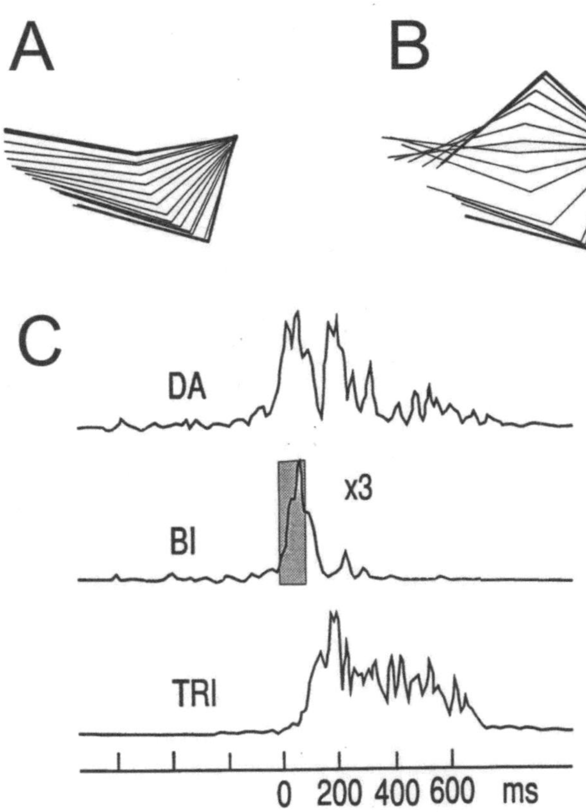

Fig. 6. DRNN simulation of the thrusting movement before (stick diagram in A) and after the artificial increase (X3) of the EMG burst of the BI muscle (stick diagram in B) (rectangular grey area in C). Note the hyperextension of the elbow induced by the BI increase.

As a biarticular muscle, the BI is able to produce an elevation of the arm. If this movement is explosive it can induce a passive but very fast extension of the forearm like in a flying effect. After the learning phase the DRNN is able to reproduce the lunging movement (Fig. 6A) and it is thus possible to use it as a simulator for testing the hypothesis that this extension movement is due to the effect of a dynamic interaction torque. The net torque is defined as the sum of all of the torques acting on a joint. In the lunging movement of the arm, the net torque acting at the elbow is equal to the sum of the gravitational, interaction, and muscle torques. In our case, the EMG bursts may be considered as a representation of the muscle torques acting on the different implicated joints and used as DRNN inputs. Bastian et al. (1996) elegantly established the inverse dynamics equations for the extension movement of the arm during a reaching task. The calculation of the net torque as the product of the moment of inertia of the involved segments and the angular acceleration around a given joint, determines the time series of joint angles and resultant limb trajectory. The angular acceleration of the shoulder and the elbow (Fig. 6B,C,F) are given here as output signals for the DRNN mapping. If the gravitational torque for the same movement remains the same regardless how fast the movement is made, in contrast the dynamic interaction torque, the passive mechanical torque generated when two or more linked segments move one another, depends greatly on joint velocity and acceleration. Like in the very fast lunging movement performed by the elite fencers, the interaction torques increase in magnitude. Thus in order to test our hypothesis that the DRNN has identified the dynamic interaction torque acting on the elbow, we have artificially increased the amplitude of the BI burst acting as the prime mover of the lunging movement (Fig. 6). When this increased BI burst (3X) was used in conjunction with the other unmodified EMG burst as input for a learned DRNN, it produced a strong reinforcement of the extension movement of the elbow. This demonstrates that the DRNN has identified the BI burst as inducing an interaction torque at the elbow joint by the production of the elevation movement of the arm. The final proof of this interaction effect should be obtained by performing inverse dynamics analysis in parallel to the DRNN simulation, but this demonstration is out of the scope of the present chapter.

6. Acknowledgements

We wish to thank T. D'Angelo, M. Dufief, E. Hortmanns, and E. Toussaint for expert technical assistance. This work was funded by the Belgian Federal Science Policy Office, the European Space Agency, (AO-2004, 118), the Belgian National Fund for Scientific Research (FNRS), the research funds of the Université Libre de Bruxelles and of the Université de Mons (Belgium), the FEDER support (BIOFACT), and the MINDWALKER project (FP7 - 2007-2013) supported by the European Commission. This paper presents research results of the Belgian Network DYSCO (Dynamical Systems, Control, and Optimization), funded by the Interuniversity Attraction Poles Programme, initiated by the Belgian State, Science Policy Office. The scientific responsibility rests with its author(s).

7. References

Bastian A.J., Martin T.A., Keating J.G., Thach W.T. (1996) Cerebellar ataxia: abnormal control of interaction torques across multiple joints. *J Neurophysiol.* 76(1):492-509.

Bengoetxea A., Dan B., Leurs F., Cebolla A.M., De Saedeleer C., Gillis P, Cheron G. (2010)

Rhythmic muscular activation pattern for fast figure-eight movement. *Clin Neurophysiol.* May;121(5):754-765.

Borghese N.A., Bianchi L., Lacquaniti F. (1996) Kinematic determinants of human locomotion. *J Physiol*;494:863-879.

Cheron, G. and Godaux, E. (1986). Long latency reflex regulation in human ballistic movement. *Human Movement Science* 5: 217-233

Cheron, G., Bengoetxea, A., Bouillot, E., Lacquaniti, F. and Dan, B. (2001a). Early emergence of temporal co-ordination of lower limb segments elevation angles in human locomotion. *Neurosi. Lett.* 308, 123-127.

Cheron G., Bouillot E., Dan B., Bengoetxea A., Draye J. P. and Lacquaniti F. (2001b). Development of a kinematic coordination pattern in toddler locomotion: planar covariation. *Exp. Brain Res.* 137, 455-466.

Cheron G., Leurs, F., Bengoetxea A., Draye J.P., Destree M. and Dan B. (2003) A dynamic recurrent neural network for multi-muscles electromyographic mapping to elevation angles of the lower limb in human locomotion. *J Neurosci. Meth.*129(2):95-104.

Cheron G, Cebolla AM, Bengoetxea A, Leurs F, Dan B. (2007) Recognition of the physiological actions of the triphasic EMG pattern by a dynamic recurrent neural network. *Neurosci Lett.* 6;414(2):192-196.

Cheron G., Cebolla A., Leurs F., Bengoetxea A. & Dan B. (2006) Development and motor control : from the first step on. In *Progress in Motor Control: Motor Control and Learning over the lifespan.* Eds ML Latash and F Lestienne, Springer pp 127-139.

Cheney P.D., Fetz E.E., Palmer S.S. (1985) Patterns of facilitation and suppression of antagonist forelimb muscles from motor cortex sites in the awake monkey. *J Neurophysiol*; 53: 805-820.

Cheron G., Draye J.P., Bourgeois M, Libert G. (1996) A dynamic neural network identification of electromyography and arm trajectory relationship during complex movements. *IEEE Trans Biomed Eng*; 43:552-558.

Cheron G., Draye J.P., Bengoetxea A., Dan B. (1999) Kinematics invariance in multi-directional complex movements in free space: effect of changing initial direction. *Clin Neurophysiol*;110: 757-64.

Doya K. (1993) Universality of fully connected recurrent neural networks. Technical report. University of California: San Diego.

Draye J.P., Pavisic D., Cheron G. and Libert G. (1995) Adaptative time constant improved the prediction capacity of recurrent neural network. *Neural Processing Letters*, 2, n°3: 1-5

Draye J.P., Pavisic D., Cheron G. and Libert G. (1996). Dynamic recurrent neural networks: a dynamical analysis. *IEEE Transactions on Systems Man, and Cybernetics* 26. 5: 692-706.

Draye J.P. Winters J.M. Cheron G. (2002) Self-selected modular recurrent neural networks with postural and inertial subnetworks applied to complex movements.*Biol. Cybern.* 87 27-39.

Edelman G. M. (1987). *Neural Darwinism.* New York: Basic Books.

Forssberg H. (1985). Ontogeny of human locomotor control. I. Infant stepping, supported locomotion and transition to independent locomotion. *Experimental Brain Research*, *57*, 480–493.

Gibson E. J. (1988). Exploratory behavior in the development of perceiving, acting, and the acquiring of knowledge. *Annual Review of Psychology, 39,* 1–41.

Hadders-Algra M. (2002). Variability in infant motor behavior: A hallmark of the healthy nervous system. *Infant Behavior and Development, 25,* 433–451.

Hadders-Algra M., Brogren, E.. and Forssberg, H. (1996). Ontogeny of postural adjustments during sitting in infancy: Variation, selection, and modulation. *Journal of Physiology, 493,* 273–288.

Hatsopoulos N.G., Paninski L and Donoghue J.P. (2003)Sequential movement representations based on correlated neuronal activity. *Exp Brain Res;* 149(4): 478-486.

Hatsopoulos N.G., Xu Q. and Amit Y. (2007) Encoding of movement fragments in the motor cortex. *J Neurosci;*27(19): 5105-2114.

Hornik K., Stinchcombe M.. and White H. (1989) Multilayer feedforward networks are universal approximators. *Neural Networks;*2:359 -366.

Ivanenko Y. P., Dominici N., Cappellini G., Dan B., Cheron G. and Lacquaniti F. (2004). Development of pendulum mechanism and kinematic coordination from the first unsupported steps in toddlers. *J. Exp. Biol.* 207, 3797-3810.

Jackson A., Gee V.J., Baker S.N.. and Lemon R.G. (2003)Synchrony between neurons with similar muscle fields in monkey motor cortex. *Neuron;* 38: 115-125.

Jackson A., Mavoori J. and Fetz E.E.(2007) Correlations between the same motor cortex cells and arm muscles during a trained task, free behavior, and natural sleep in the macaque monkey. *J Neurophysiol;* 97(1):360-374.

Kelso J. A. S. (1995). *Dynamic patterns: The self-organization of brain and behavior.* Cambridge, MA: MIT Press.

Koike Y. and, Kawato M. (1994) Estimation of arm posture in 3D-Space from surface EMG signals using a neural network model. *IEICE Trans Inf Syst;*E77-D:368-375.

Koike Y. and Kawato M. (1995) Estimation of dynamic joint torques and trajectory formation from surface electromyography signals using a neural network model. Biol Cybern;73:291_/300.

Lacquaniti F., Grasso R.. and Zago M. (1999) Motor patterns in walking. *News Physiol Sci* 1999;14:168_/74.

Ledebt A. (2000). Changes in arm posture during the early acquisition of walking. *Infant Behavior and Development, 23,* 79–89.

Okamoto T..and Goto Y. (1985). Human infant pre-independent and independent walking. In S. Kondo (Ed.), *Primate morphophysiology, locomotor analyses and human bipedalism.* University of Tokyo Press Tokyo pp. 25–45.:.

Okamoto T. and Okamoto, K. (2001). Electromyographic characteristics at the onset of independent walking in infancy. *Electromyography and Clinical Neurophysiology, 41,* 33–41.

Okamoto T., Okamoto, K., and Andrew, P. D. (2003). Electromyography developmental changes in one individual from newborn stepping to mature walking. *Gait and Posture, 17,* 18–27.

Rubino D., Robbins K.A. and Hatsopoulos NG. (2006) Propagating waves mediate information transfer in the motor cortex. *Nat Neurosci;* 9(12):1549-1557.

Silva F.M. and Almeida L.B. (1990) Speeding up backpropagation In Eckmiller, ed. *Advanced Neural Computer* . Amsterdam, Elsevier, pp. 151-158.

Schwartz A.B. and Moran D.W. (1999) Motor cortical activity during drawing movements: population representation during lemniscate tracing. *J Neurophysiol*; 82: 2705-2718.

Sanes J.N. and Truccolo W. (2003) Motor "binding:" do functional assemblies in primary motor cortex have a role? *Neuron*; 10; 38(1): 3-5.

Savelberg H.C.. and Herzog W. (1997) Prediction of dynamic tendon forces from electromyographic signals: an artificial neural network approach. *J Neurosci Methods*;78:65 -74.

Sepulveda F., Wells D.M.. and Vaughan C.L. (1993) A neural network representation of electromyography and joint dynamics in human gait. *J Biomech*;26:101-109.

Sporns O..and Edelman G.M. (1993) Solving Bernstein's problem: a proposal for the development of coordinated movement by selection. *Child Dev.* 64(4):960-981.

Thelen E.. and Corbetta D. (1994) Exploration and selection in the early acquisition of skill. *Int Rev Neurobiol.*;37:75-102; discussion 121-123.

Turvey M.T. and Fitzpatrick P. (1993) Commentary: development of perception-action systems and general principles of pattern formation. *Child Dev.* ;64(4):1175-90.

Tsuboshita Y., and Okamoto H. (2007) Context-dependent retrieval of information by neural-network dynamics with continuous attractors. *Neural Netw.* ;20(6):705-713.

6

Compact Internal Representation as a Functional Basis for Protocognitive Exploration of Dynamic Environments

Valeri A. Makarov and José Antonio Villacorta-Atienza
Universidad Complutense de Madrid
Spain

1. Introduction

Nature has provided living beings with a set of cognitive properties that enables subjective perception of the external world with the aim of constructing behaviors and survival within specific environments. A simple but comprehensive example is a near-range searching for a target by a mobile agent in a time-evolving environment. It requires fast and reliable generation of flexible behaviors that must take into account not only the current state of the environment and of the agent, but also infer on their future states.

Despite a vast literature and numerous contexts where the concept of cognition appears [see, e.g., (Baars & Gage, 2010; Newell, 1994; Wasserman & Zentall, 2009)], there is no generally accepted functional definition. Nevertheless capacities such as *Internal Representation* (IR) of the external world, memory, and learning are commonly accepted as elements constituting cognition (Godfrey-Smith, 2001). For the study of the problem of cognitive exploration of dynamic environments it seems sensible to restrict the cognitive abilities to those manifested externally in motricity, i.e. to those experimentally verifiable in animal models. Then we can speak about "initial stages" of cognition or protocognition, a subject that has been for decades a hot spot both in theoretical and experimental (mainly in insects and mammals) research [see, e.g., (Cruse, 2003; Hesslow, 2002; Newell, 1994) and references therein]. In this chapter as a working hypothesis we use a general functional definition of protocognition as the basis levels of the "Cognitive Pyramid" given by Wray et al. (2007). Namely, the protocognitive capacities organize the sensory information into structured representations, which provide "skeletal subsolutions" for the higher cognitive levels.

The complexity of protocognitive skills stems from several factors shared by living beings. First, an enormous amount of sensory information must be structured and broken into aspects relevant for the aim-driven perception (e.g., position and shape of a target), while discarding the rest. Usually this is done by the agent's sensory system, which provides highly specialized information to the central nervous system (Bear et al., 2007; Kandel et al., 2000). Second, a serious source of complexity is the continuous evolution of the environment and causal relations among its constituents. This requires anticipation and hence a predictive model of the environment and of the agent itself. The cognitive neuronal pathways or circuits are in charge of building up forward world models based on genetic wiring and experience. Then the external input modulates the (nonlinear) dynamics of the neuronal circuits, which produce behaviors ready to be selected by upper cognitive levels (e.g., using motivation) and to be enacted. Third, an efficient (fast, reliable, and flexible) management of behavioral problems relies on memorization of novel situations and learning associations with corresponding successful behaviors. Libraries of stereotypic situations can significantly speedup the agent's reaction and make automatic the previously learned behaviors converting them into subconscious states. An example is an experiment with astronauts catching a ball under reduced effective gravity (McIntyre et al., 2001). At the beginning of the experiment the peak of anticipatory muscle activation occurred earlier than the real impact of the ball, which lead to incorrect, biased by the experience in the Earth, behaviors. However, after a few days the astronauts adapted to the new conditions, i.e. the inner mental "model of the ball trajectory" successfully learned new parameters and finally were able to "calculate" reliably and fast the necessary movement.

It is noteworthy that the first two features set the ground level of the Cognitive Pyramid, whereas the third one belongs to the intermediate floor and operates over the information provided by the ground level. Then intriguing questions are: what are the basic principles of organization and operation of the cognitive pathways? and how can we mimic them? An answer to these questions, besides its theoretical value, also would enable a qualitative advance in mobile robotics.

Here we develop a paradigm of protocognitive neuronal pathways involved into exploration of dynamic environments based on the so-called principle of *Compact Internal Representations* (CIRs) of interactions between the agent and its environment (Villacorta-Atienza et al., 2010). Based on recent experimental hints we hypothesize that brain, for effective representation of time-evolving situations, may use specific time-space transformation that reduces the corresponding time-dependent structures into static patterns that can be easily compared, stored, and organized into "libraries". Then the protocognitive pathways should include several basic elements:

i) Preliminary sensory blocks, capable of extracting the information essential for prediction of the future states of the environment;

ii) A substrate responsible for the IR, which models a set of virtual futures induced by agent's decisions (e.g., collisions with obstacles in the time-space domain);

iii) Working memory that is used for learning and storing the previous successful experiences, which can optimize and speedup the decision making.

In Sect. 2 we show how the modeling of time-space collisions can be implemented in a *two-dimensional* (2D) neuronal network. The network, called *Causal Neural Network* (CNN), exploits in a mental world model the principle of causality, which enables reduction of the time-dependent structure of real dynamic situations to compact static patterns. A single point in the multidimensional phase space of the CNN gives a CIR of the dynamic situation. Such CIR provides complete description of the time-space collisions. A remarkable feature of CIRs is that they do not merely represent situations in which the agent is involved, but contain a set of behaviors adapted to these specific situations. These behaviors can be used as a basic entities in higher cognitive activity to create new solutions. In consequence CIR may be considered as a functional basis for protocognition.

In Sect. 3 we study how individual memory items can be stored assuming that situations given in the environment can be represented in the form of synaptic-like couplings in a *Recurrent Neural Network* (RNN). We provide theoretical analysis illustrating the learning process and response to novel or incomplete stimuli and show that RNN is suitable for

simulation of working memory. Furthermore, we show that a similar RNN can be specially trained to perform algebraic operations over the input stimuli. This ability is essential for prediction of trajectories of moving objects, i.e. for modeling of future states of the environment.
In Sect. 4 we provide a general architecture of a protocognitive agent, which includes conscious and subconscious pathways builded up on the basis of the neuronal networks discussed in Sects. 2 and 3. Then we illustrate generation of behaviors and their learning by the agent moving in realistic time-evolving environments. Special attention is given to dynamical construction of libraries of stereotypic situations and associated CIRs. We show how, based on the initial sensory information only, the agent can retrieve an appropriate CIR from the library and hence make fast and efficient decision.
Finally in Sect. 5 we summarize our results.

2. Compact internal representation of complex environments

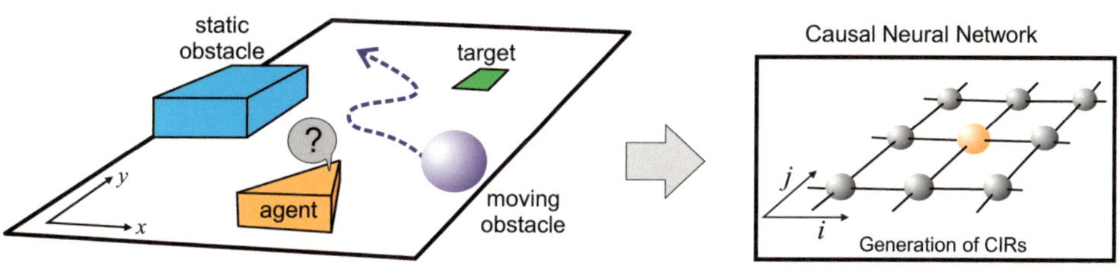

Fig. 1. Sketch of an arena containing an agent, a target, and static and moving obstacles. The agent perceives all objects in the arena and makes a decision on how to reach the target avoiding collisions with the obstacles. The decision making is based on Compact Internal Representations (CIRs) of itself and of the environment created in the Causal Neural Network.

Internal Representation is a task-oriented inner description of the environment and of the agent itself, which offers distinct modes to fulfill a task. In what follows we discuss one specific decision making problem: a search for paths to a target by a mobile agent in a time-evolving environment (Fig. 1). For the sake of simplicity the target is considered immobile and can be an object or a specific place or even an area in the arena. We assume that the target and obstacles emit or reflect a signal, e.g., sound or light, which is perceived by the agent's sensory system, and hence the agent can make a non-blind decision.
To avoid obstacles (especially moving) the agent may construct a spatiotemporal IR of the observed dynamic situation and use it as a "world model" to resolve collisions. Such time-dependent IR should be based on prediction of the possible positions of the obstacles and of the agent in the (mental) future. However, time-dependent IRs due to their excessive complexity are not suitable for protocognitive behavior. A big challenge is to understand how the brain makes compact and efficient descriptions of time-evolving situations. In this section we describe an approach that enables reduction of time-dependent IRs to CIRs, i.e. to static patterns (Villacorta-Atienza et al., 2010). These static patterns emerge in the so-called Causal Neural Network (CNN), whose dynamics is driven by the sensory information (Fig. 1). Geometrically the CNN is an $(n \times m)$-lattice of locally coupled neurons. The lattice coordinates (i, j) scale to real coordinates (x, y) in the arena.

2.1 Static environments

Let us first briefly describe how CIR can be created in the simplest case when all elements in a 2D arena (except the agent) are immobile. Then the sensory output is time independent, and hence the immobile obstacles and the target can be simply mapped into the corresponding cells in the CNN. The CNN models the process of *virtual (mental) exploration* of the environment by the agent. Conceptually, a number of identical virtual agents are released at the agent's initial position (orange cell in Fig. 1) and perform a random search in the lattice space until they explore completely the "arena" or some of them reach the target's image in the CNN. Then the distribution of the virtual agents in the CNN lattice defines the CIR, which further can be used for path planing.

The dynamics of the CNN (for static environment) is given by:

$$\dot{r}_{ij} = d\Delta r_{ij} - r_{ij}p_{ij} \tag{1}$$

where r_{ij} is the neuronal state variable, representing the concentration of virtual agents at the cell (i,j); the time derivative is taken with respect to the *mental* (inner) time τ; $\Delta r_{ij} = r_{i+1,j} + r_{i-1,j} + r_{i,j+1} + r_{i,j-1} - 4r_{ij}$ denotes the discrete Laplace operator describing the local (nearest neighbor) interneuronal couplings, whose strength is controlled by d; and p_{ij} accounts for the target:

$$p_{ij} = \begin{cases} 1, & \text{if } (i,j) \text{ is occupied by target} \\ 0, & \text{otherwise} \end{cases} \tag{2}$$

It is worth pointing out that a target is not a real entity existing in the environment (as an object or place), instead it is designated by the agent's motivation layer. For example, a football player can turn aside from or catch a ball depending on which side he plays on. Thus the target is not an external constraint but an internal emergent property of the brain, whose influence we model by the reactive term in (1). This differs from other approaches that postulate targets as singular elements in the environment [see, e.g., (Schmidt & Azarm, 1992)].

Obstacles are external constraints whose biological identity, provided by boundary cells (Savelli et al., 2008), suggests that they shape the IR through altering states of the neurons corresponding to the obstacle boundaries. We assume that the obstacles are solid non-penetrable objects, hence a virtual agent reaching an obstacle frontier rebounds and continues exploring the arena. Thus we impose zero-flux (Neumann) boundary conditions at the obstacle's frontiers and also at the arena boundary.

At $\tau = 0$ no virtual agent exists, hence we set $r_{ij}(0) = 0$ for all CNN cells except those occupied by the agent, where $r_{ij}(\tau) = r_a$ for $\tau \geq 0$. It has been shown that stable steady states are the only attractors in the phase space $\Psi = \mathbb{R}_+^{nm}$ of the CNN (Villacorta-Atienza et al., 2010). Thus any trajectory in Ψ defined by initial conditions (except a null set) tends to one of the stable steady states $\{r_{ij}^*\} \in \Psi$, which is the CIR of the given static situation. By unfolding this steady state into the three-dimensional lattice space $\{\mathbb{Z}^2, \mathbb{R}_+\}$ we get a 2D stationary pattern that can be used to trace paths starting at the agent location and crossing the contour lines. We note that r_{ij}^* satisfies the discrete Laplace equation, and consequently the created pattern has no local minimums (Keymeulen & Decuyper, 1994; Louste & Liegeois, 2000). This ensures that all paths (except a null set) derived from this approach end at the target, and hence we obtain multiple alternatives to reach the target.

To illustrate the approach we simulated a 2D arena consisting of an agent, two immobile obstacles, and a target (Fig. 2, left). The corresponding sensory information has been used to integrate numerically the CNN model. Figure 2 (right) shows the limit pattern $\{r_{ij}^*\}$

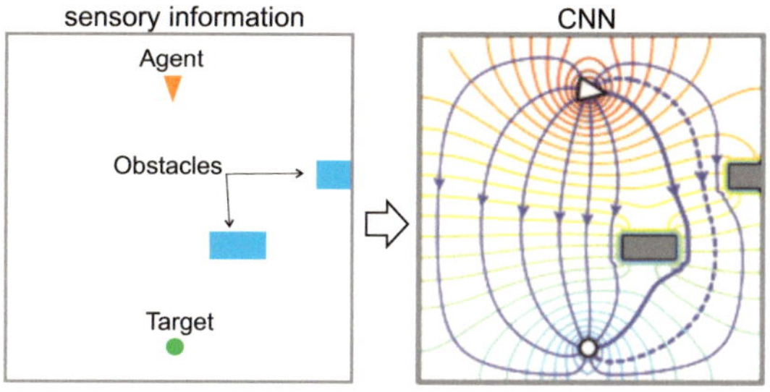

Fig. 2. Compact Internal Representation of static environments. Left panel: 2D arena consisting of an agent (red triangle), immobile obstacles (blue rectangles), and a target (green circle). Positions of all objects are mapped into the CNN whose relaxation yields a CIR, i.e. a static 2D pattern $\{r_{ij}^*\}_{i,j=1}^{60}$. Right panel: Contour plot of $\{r_{ij}^*\}$ (colored curves from red to cyan). A set of paths start at the agent's position and descend down the gradient to the target (blue arrowed curves). The agent is free to chose among different alternatives, e.g., by minimizing the path length (solid thick curve) or by rising safety (dashed curve), under additional constraint that it must pass between the two obstacles. Parameter values: $r_a = 1$, $d = 2.5$, and the integration time $\tau_{end} = 10^3$.

(distribution of virtual agents). We notice that there exist multiple curves connecting the agent and the target locations. Thus the obtained CIR offers a freedom to chose among different alternatives. We also notice that the pattern has smooth transitions between actual obstacles and empty space. This accounts for uncertainty in the obstacle dimensions and positions. Then path planning from the agent to the target can naturally include the level of safety, e.g., a cost function that describes the risk of collision against the length of the path. The strategy can also include additional conditions, such as to pass through the gap between two obstacles (dashed curve vs thick solid curve in Fig. 2).

2.2 Dynamic environments

The above discussed CIR of static environments cannot be applied directly to dynamic situations. However, we shall show now how the moving obstacles can be mapped into static images in the CNN lattice space, and hence the problem can be reduced to the *effectively* static case.

To illustrate the concept let us consider an arena with a single moving obstacle (Fig. 3A). As in the static case at $\tau = 0$ virtual agents are released into the CNN and start exploring the environment, which yields a wavefront composed of those virtual agents that reached the points furthest away from the agent initial position. The wavefront can be viewed as the "present" in the mental time τ, dividing the three dimensional spacetime into two disjoint sets corresponding to the points in the mental past (part of the lattice visited by virtual agents) and in the future (part to be visited) (Fig. 3B). Thus all neurons inside the area enclosed by the wavefront belong to the virtual past and those outside the area belong to the virtual future.

Due to the *principle of causality* none of the events occurring ahead of the wavefront (in the virtual future) can affect those behind it (in the virtual past). This allows restricting the predicted motion of the obstacle (and hence collisions possible in the virtual future) to the lattice space outward the wavefront (Fig. 3B, gray vs blue obstacle parts). As the mental time τ proceeds, a circular wavefront expands until the obstacle will be reached. The spatial locations where the wavefront coincides with the obstacle (Fig. 3B, yellow circle) correspond to agent-obstacle collisions in the virtual present that should be avoided at the

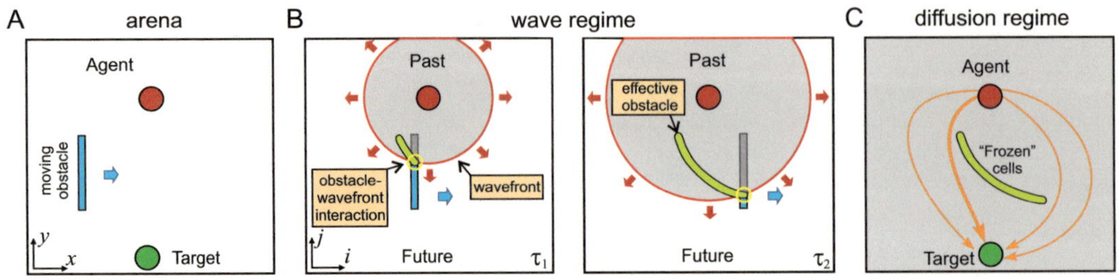

Fig. 3. The concept of CIR of a dynamic situation. A) 2D arena consists of an agent (red circle), a target (green circle), and a moving obstacle (blue rectangle). B) Three dimensional spacetime plots sketching the wave regime in the CNN. The expanding wavefront separates the agent virtual past from the future (gray and white areas, respectively). Effective influence of the moving obstacle over the agent is restricted to the isochronous spatiotemporal points of the wavefront and moving obstacle (yellow circle). This encloses a set of frozen neurons (green area), which form the effective obstacle. C) The diffusion regime (behind the wavefront) as in Fig. 2B shapes the CIR of the dynamic situation and enables decision making.

motor execution. With the time course these spatial locations (forbidden to be visited by the agent) delimit a set of neurons (Fig. 3B, green area), which progressively leads to formation of a static *effective* obstacle. Since these neurons belong to the virtual past, new events cannot change their state, hence their dynamics can be "frozen". Thus the principle of causality in the IR context converts moving obstacles into time-independent effective obstacles.
Once the effective obstacle has been formed and the wavefront has passed, the IR problem reduces to the previous static case. Hence we can apply the approach illustrated in Fig. 2. Then the steady state pattern $\{r_{ij}^*\}$ obtained for the new effectively static situation gives a CIR of the dynamic situation and ensures that all feasible paths will avoid the moving obstacle (Fig. 3C). Thus CIRs of dynamic situations are obtained in two steps:

1. Wave regime. Propagation of a wavefront separating the virtual future from the virtual past. Effective obstacles are formed in the CNN lattice.
2. Diffusion regime. Evolution of the CNN with effective (immobile) obstacles shapes the CIR.

Note that both regimes occur simultaneously in the virtual mental time, but belong to different spatial regions in the CNN lattice.

2.3 The model of CNN

The complete model of the CNN is based on the lattice described in Sect. 2.1, but now each unit is a modified FitzHugh-Nagumo neuron, which yields the following dynamical system (Villacorta-Atienza et al., 2010):

$$\begin{aligned} \dot{r}_{ij} &= q_{ij}\left(H(r_{ij})\left[f(r_{ij}) - v_{ij}\right] + d\Delta r_{ij} - r_{ij}p_{ij}\right) \\ \dot{v}_{ij} &= (r_{ij} - 7v_{ij} - 2)/25 \end{aligned} \tag{3}$$

where v_{ij} is the so-called recovery variable; $f(r)$ is a cubic nonlinearity, which for numerical simulations we set to $f(r) = (-r^3 + 4r^2 - 2r - 2)/7$; and H is the regime controlling

(Heaviside step) function:

$$H(r) = \begin{cases} 1, & \text{if } r \le r_{\text{h}} \\ 0, & \text{otherwise} \end{cases}$$

where r_{h} is the threshold separating the wave and diffusion regimes.
The binary variable $q_{ij}(\tau) \in \{0,1\}$ in (3) describes the influence of effective obstacles (green area in Fig. 3B) on the CNN dynamics. This inhibitory term mimicks the possible effect that border cells may exert over the activity of grid cells (Savelli et al., 2008). At $\tau = 0$ no effective obstacle exists and $q_{ij}(0) = 1, \forall(i,j)$. For $\tau > 0$ a concentric circular wave (sketched in Fig. 3B) is generated. Once the wavefront catches up an obstacle (mobile or immobile) it slips around. Cells, where the wavefront "touches" obstacle at $\tau = \tau_{\text{tch}}$ (Fig. 3B, yellow circle) become "frozen", $q_{ij}(\tau \ge \tau_{\text{tch}}) = 0$. As a consequence, for the frozen cells we have

$$r_{ij}(\tau) = r_{ij}(\tau_{\text{tch}}), \text{ for } \tau \ge \tau_{\text{tch}} \text{ and } (i,j) \text{ frozen} \tag{4}$$

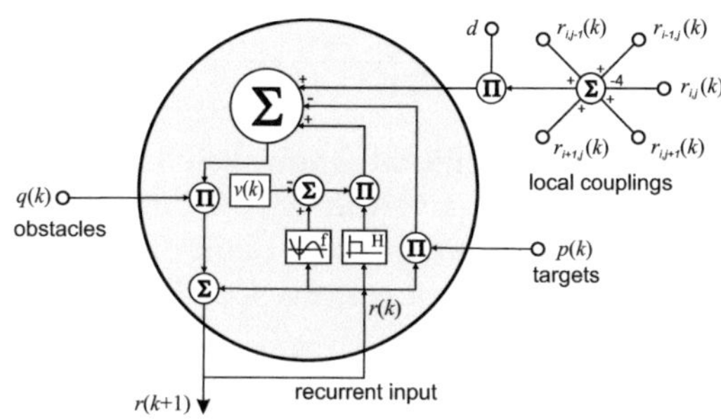

Fig. 4. Circuit implementation of the modified FitzHugh-Nagumo neuronal unit used in the CNN lattice (3). The blocks f, H, Σ, and Π stand for cubic nonlinearity, Heaviside step function, sum, and product, respectively. The block $v(k)$ updates the state of the corresponding recovery variable (linear sum of $r(k)$ and $v(k)$).

Figure 4 shows the circuit implementation of the CNN unit operating in the discrete time k. The unit, besides its own recurrent feedback $r_{ij}(k)$, receives three types of inputs: i) local coupling from the nearest neighbors, ii) inhibitory signal modeling the presence of effective obstacles $q_{ij}(k)$ (provided by a recurrent neural network described in Sect. 3.2), and iii) motivational input defining target locations $p_{ij}(k)$ (given by Eq. (2)). The updated state $r_{ij}(k+1)$ is readout at the unit output.
It can be shown that the unit's intrinsic dynamics (for $d = 0$, $p = 0$, $q = 1$, and $H = 1$) is bistable, with two stable steady states at $r_{\text{d}} = 0$ and $r_{\text{u}} = 3$. For low enough coupling strength $d < d_{\text{cr}}$ this yields multi-stability and even spatial chaos (Nekorkin & Makarov, 1995; Nekorkin et al., 1997; Sepulchre & MacKay, 1997). The upstate r_{u} has much bigger basin of attraction than the downstate r_{d}. For a strong coupling $d > d_{\text{cr}}$ by fixing just a single neuron in the upstate we create a wave that propagates with a constant velocity and switch all neurons from the downstate to the upstate. Hence to obtain a wavefront in our problem we select high enough inter-neuronal coupling $d > d_{\text{cr}}$.
The propagating wave switches neurons to the upstate and hence $H = 0$ and also $q_{ij} = const$ behind the wavefront. For long enough $\tau > \tau^*$ the wave will explore all the CNN space and (3) will reduce to (1). Thus (3) also exhibits the gradient property for $\tau > \tau^*$ (Villacorta-Atienza et al., 2010), although its transient process is not gradient. Thus trajectories in the phase space $\Psi = \mathbb{R}_+^{NM} \times \mathbb{R}^{NM}$ of the CNN (3) tend to one of the stable steady states that defines the CIR for a given dynamic situation.

We notice that once the wavefront reaches the target image in the CNN at $\tau = \tau_{tr}$ the calculations can be stopped. Then by construction there exists at least one path starting from the agent position and ending at the target. Thus we get a first suitable approximation to the CIR. Running the CNN further for $\tau > \tau_{tr}$ improves the shaping of the $\{r_{ij}\}$ pattern in $\{\mathbb{Z}^2, \mathbb{R}_+\}$, which leads to an exponentially saturating optimization of paths.

2.4 Numerical simulations

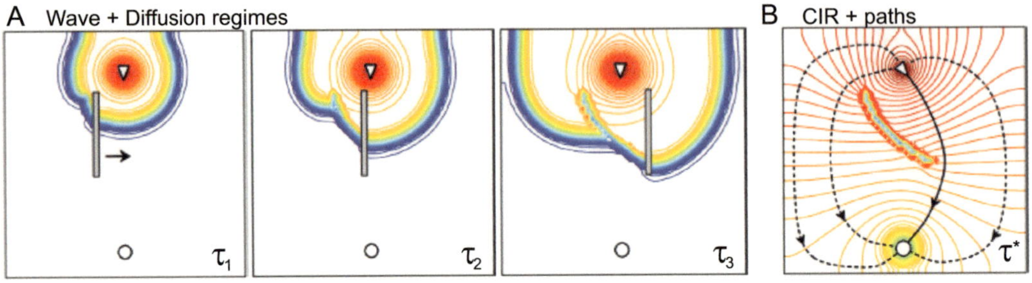

Fig. 5. Formation of the CIR of the dynamic situation sketched in Fig. 3A. A) Three successive snapshots illustrate how the wavefront (dense blue curves) is affected by the virtual motion of the obstacle. Colored curves show equipotential profiles of $r_{ij}(\tau_k)$, $k = 1, 2, 3$. B) Final CIR after the diffusion phase. Black solid curve is the shortest path to the target. Dashed paths are safer but longer.

We simulated numerically the dynamic situation sketched in Fig. 3A[1]. After observing the object during the first time steps (needed for the estimation of its initial velocity and acceleration) its future trajectory can be predicted (we discuss this problem in Sect. 3). This calculation is fed into the CNN. Figure 5A shows three successive snapshots of the CNN state (2D profile of $\{r_{ij}\}$) where for convenience we also have drawn the virtual positions of the obstacle (gray bar). The obstacle's virtual movement affects the wavefront propagating outward the target position. The lattice units, where the spatiotemporal positions of the wavefront and of the obstacle image match, correspond to effective obstacles and their dynamics is frozen (curved area behind the obstacle in Fig. 5A).
Behind the wavefront the network dynamics switches to the diffusion phase, which finally shapes the $\{r_{ij}\}$ pattern. This shaping does not affect the frozen cells (effective obstacles), instead virtual agents "diffuse" around them thus finding all possible ways and eventually end up at the target. Thus for a big enough τ^* the profile $\{r_{ij}(\tau^*)\}$ creates a purpose-based CIR of the dynamic situation where the potential agent motions are synchronized with the moving obstacle (Fig. 5B).
As it has been discussed above, the CIR offers multiple alternatives on how to reach the target. For example, the agent (e.g., being in a hurry) can chose the shortest path to the target (solid curve in Fig. 5B), or select a longer but safer path (dashed curves in Fig. 5B).

3. RNNs as elements for CIR-memory and prediction of trajectories

In the previous section we described how CIRs of complex time-evolving situations can be created. Such process involves modeling of trajectories of moving obstacles. In this section

[1] The corresponding video and more examples can be found at http://www.mat.ucm.es/~vmakarov/IRNN.html

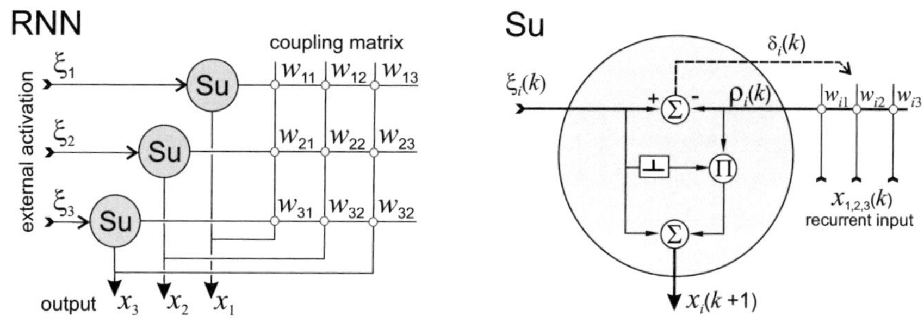

Fig. 6. Circuit implementation of a neural network (case $n = 3$) composed of recurrently coupled Suppression Units (*Su*). Blocks marked by Σ and Π perform input summation and multiplication, respectively. The other block (turned over "T") is a nonlinear element with sketched transduction characteristic.

we shall show that the modeling can be accomplished by a specially trained recurrent neural network. Besides RNNs can be used for effective storing and retrieval of frequently appearing CIRs.

3.1 Universal network model

The networks considered in this section consist of n recurrently connected "suppression" units or neurons (Fig. 6). The units operate in a discrete time $k \in \mathbb{Z}$, linked to the mental time $\tau = kh$ (h is an inner time scale of the agent that may vary between "species" and/or "individuals"). Each neuron has an external input denoted as signal $\xi_i(k)$, which we also call activation, an internal (recurrent) input $\rho_i(k)$, and an output $x_i(k+1)$. Thus the network state and its inputs are, in general, time-dependent nD column vectors, i.e. $x, \xi, \rho \in \mathbb{R}^n \times \mathbb{Z}$.[2]
The recurrent input is given by a weighted sum of the output of all units in the network

$$\rho_i(k) = \sum_{j=1}^{n} w_{ij} x_j(k) \tag{5}$$

where the matrix $W = (w_{ij}), w_{ij} \in \mathbb{R}, \forall i, j = 1, \ldots, n$ describes the inter-neuron (synaptic-like) couplings. As we shall show further the network can learn different static and time-evolving situations by an appropriate adjustment of the coupling matrix W. Learning rules can be described as teacher forcing based on the classical delta rule using the mismatch between the internal and external inputs (K'uhn et al., 2007; Makarov et al., 2008):

$$\delta_i(k) = \xi_i(k) - \rho_i(k)$$

We shall consider two RNNs with the same inner structure (Fig. 1), but responsible for different tasks:

1. Learning and prediction of trajectories of moving objects (Sect. 3.2)
2. Learning and retrieval of CIRs (Sect. 3.3)

The difference in their behaviors is achieved by different learning rules, which in turn produce the connectivity patterns (matrices W) that finally decide how each network interprets the external stimuli.

[2] As usual for any two vectors $x, y \in \mathbb{R}^n$ we define a scalar product: $\langle x, y \rangle \equiv x^T y$ (T denotes transpose). Then $\|x\| = \sqrt{\langle x, x \rangle}$ is the norm or length of the vector x.

3.1.1 Operational phase

In the operational phase the coupling matrix W is fixed (e.g., after preceding learning or due to genetic wiring) and the RNN is exposed to a novel stimulus $\xi(k)$ and produces an output $x(k)$. There is no difference between the RNNs used for trajectory modeling and CIR-memory. In *Su* the recurrent signal is suppressed and replaced by the external input if the latter is different from zero, or otherwise sent unchanged to the output

$$x_i(k+1) = \begin{cases} \xi_i(k), & \text{if } \xi_i(k) \neq 0 \\ \rho_i(k), & \text{otherwise} \end{cases} \tag{6}$$

Thus to get a nontrivial behavior, at least part of the external activation (stimulus) must be equal to zero.

3.1.2 Learning phase

During learning the network is exposed to training stimuli, i.e. to a sequence of nD vectors $\xi(k)$, $k = 0, 1, 2, \ldots$ According to the task (learning CIRs or trajectories) we distinguish two types of situations to be learned. One is so called *static situations*, when external stimuli presented to the network are assumed to be (temporarily) independent pieces of a "global picture" or simply different static patterns. A set of CIRs is an example. Then the learning does not depend on the sequence of stimuli. The other, *dynamic situations*, are characterized by essentially time dependent stimuli, i.e. stimuli composed of different vectors $\xi(1), \xi(2), \ldots$ whose sequence now indeed matters. Such stimuli can be, for example, position of a moving object in consecutive time instants.

For simplicity[3], we assume that the network training starts from zero initial conditions, i.e. $W(0) = 0$. Besides, during the training the network has no internal dynamics, i.e. (6) is reduced to $x(k+1) = \xi(k)$, which is indeed true if $\xi(k) \neq 0$.

The training is deemed finished when the total squared error $\sum \delta_i^2$ falls below a threshold. To quantify the learning performance we shall also use the normalized inter-matrix distance

$$d(k) = \frac{\|W(k) - W_\infty\|}{\|W_\infty\|} \tag{7}$$

where $W_\infty = \lim_{k\to\infty} W(k)$ is the limit (learned) matrix.

3.2 RNN modeling trajectories of moving objects

An accurate prediction of trajectories of moving objects by living beings results from previous learning (McIntyre et al., 2001), i.e. tracking of moving objects tunes a neural network responsible for the prediction. In this section we show how an RNN can be used for this purpose.

3.2.1 Trajectory model: RNN's viewpoint

From the RNN's viewpoint trajectory of a moving object can be viewed as a time dependent stimulus, i.e. an external activation of RNN (Fig. 6). Then the RNN's inner structure (strengths of interneuron couplings) should be appropriately tuned in such a way that next time, giving to the RNN initial conditions of an object, it would be able to generate its whole trajectory.

Let $s(t) = (x(t), y(t))^T$ be a 2D-trajectory[4] of motion of an object that passes at $t = 0$ through a point (x_0, y_0). Then the prediction or modeling of the object trajectory consists in estimating

---

[3] Results for a general case can be found in (Makarov et al., 2008).

[4] Extension to 3D is straightforward.

a function $\hat{s}(\tau) = (\hat{x}(\tau), \hat{y}(\tau))^T$ that approximates $s(t)$ for $t \geq 0$ based on the observation of its past (i.e. knowing $s(t)$ for $t \leq 0$ construct $\hat{s}(\tau)$ such that $\hat{s}(t) \approx s(t)$ for $t > 0$). We note that the trajectory modeling actually is made in the mental time τ.
Developing $s(t)$ into a Taylor series we obtain:

$$s(t) = s(0) + s'(0)t + \frac{s''(0)}{2}t^2 + \cdots \tag{8}$$

where $s(0) = (x_0, y_0)^T$, $s'(0) = (v_0, u_0)^T$, and $s''(0) = (a_0, b_0)^T$ are the object's position, velocity, and acceleration at $t = 0$, respectively. The time derivatives (s' and s'') are estimated (by the sensory system) from the object past ($t \leq 0$). We note that in the r.h.s. of (8) one can keep an arbitrary number of high order terms. However, their estimates require additional computational load and may not be reliable, since the error increases with the order. Thus for the x-component of $\hat{s}(\tau)$ (similar for y) in the discrete time $\tau = kh$ we define the following model:

$$\hat{x}(k) = x_0 + v_0 kh + \frac{a_0}{2}k^2h^2, \quad k \geq 0 \tag{9}$$

This model has three parameters x_0, v_0, and a_0 completely describing the observed dynamic situation. Consequently, a three-neuron RNN is required for the simulation of such dynamic situations. Besides parameters, (9) includes an inner time scale h that may vary between "species" and/or "individuals", hence its value must be tuned during the learning.

3.2.2 Learning phase: Universal structure of W_∞

During learning the RNN is exposed to training stimuli. By a training stimulus we understand a sequence of 3D vectors $\xi(k) = (x(k), v(k), a(k))^T$, which represent a piece of an observed trajectory and aren't exchangeable. Here

$$v(k) = \frac{x(k) - x(k-1)}{h}, \quad a(k) = \frac{v(k) - v(k-1)}{h} \tag{10}$$

are estimates of the velocity and acceleration provided by the sensory system from the tracking the object's position. In (Makarov et al., 2008) we have shown that such a dynamic situation can be learned by using the following learning rule:

$$W(k+1) = W(k)\left(I - \varepsilon\xi(k-1)\xi^T(k-1)\right) + \varepsilon\xi(k)\xi^T(k-1) \tag{11}$$

We notice that at each step the updating of the coupling matrix W uses two 3D vectors $\xi(k)$ and $\xi(k-1)$, and evaluation of each vector requires three time steps. Thus the minimal training sequence of vectors consists of four time steps: $\xi(1), \ldots, \xi(4)$. Then the limit matrix is given by (Makarov et al., 2008; Villacorta-Atienza et al., 2010):

$$W_\infty = \left(\xi(2), \xi(3), \xi(4)\right)\left(\xi(1), \xi(2), \xi(3)\right)^{-1} \tag{12}$$

which yields

$$W_\infty = \begin{pmatrix} 1 & h & h^2 \\ 0 & 1 & h \\ 0 & 0 & 1 \end{pmatrix} \tag{13}$$

Remarkably (13) does not depend on the particular trajectory but includes the inner time constant h only. This means that the structure of learned interneuron couplings is universal and during training the RNN can be supplied with arbitrary trajectories. Thus by tracking different trajectories of different moving objects the RNN learns the correct structure of interneuron couplings.

3.2.3 Modeling trajectories

Once the learning has been fulfilled, the RNN can be used for the prediction of trajectories. Let us assume that at $t = 0$ an object has the following parameters x_0, v_0, and a_0. At this instant the sensory system provides initial conditions to the network at $k = 0$ and then the external activation is reset to zero:

$$\xi(0) = (\bar{x}_0, \bar{v}_0, \bar{a}_0)^T \quad \text{and} \quad \xi(k) = 0, \; k > 0 \tag{14}$$

where

$$\bar{x}_0 = x_0, \qquad \bar{v}_0 = v_0 - \frac{1}{2} h a_0, \qquad \bar{a}_0 = a_0$$

are the estimates given by the sensory system. We note that the estimate of the velocity has an error due to the finite difference approximation of the time derivative (10). The corresponding trajectory is read out at the network output given by $\hat{x}(k+1) = W\hat{x}(k)$. Using (13) and (14) we obtain:

$$\hat{x}(k) = x_0 + v_0 kh + \frac{1}{2} a_0 k^2 h^2$$

Thus, although the initial conditions were not exact, the trained RNN generates a trajectory with no error.

3.2.4 Numerical simulations

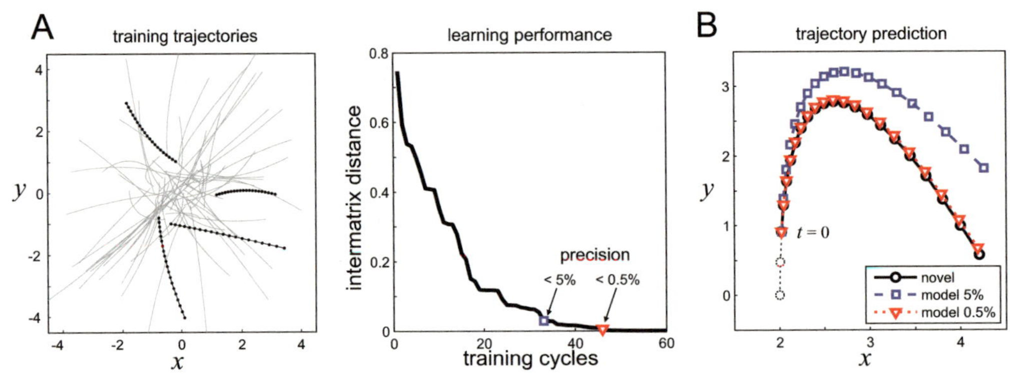

Fig. 7. Simulation of learning and modeling of trajectories by three-neuron RNN. A) Learning phase. Left panel: trajectories of moving objects used for learning (four of them are shown in black). Right panel: The learning process converges to the theoretically derived matrix (13) nearly exponentially with the number of training trajectories presented during the learning. Parameter values: $h = 0.1$, $\varepsilon = 0.1$. B) Modeling phase. A novel trajectory (black cycles) has been generated and then modeled by the RNN trained up to 5% (blue squares) and 0.5% (red triangles) precision. The first two points (dashed cycles) were used for evaluation of the initial object's velocity and acceleration (10).

To crosscheck the theoretical predictions and illustrate the trajectory learning and modeling we simulated 60 trajectories ($t \in [0, 2]$) with randomly chosen parameters, i.e. acceleration, initial velocity and position (Fig. 7A, left panel). The trajectories have been discretized ($h = 0.1$) and submitted to the RNN for training. Figure 7A (right panel) shows the learning performance, i.e. the evolution of the intermatrix distance (7) between $W(k)$ and the theoretically predicted matrix (13). During the training $W(k)$ converges to W_∞ and the error decreases below 5% and 0.5% in about 35 and 45 stimulus presentations, respectively.

Once the learning was deemed finished (with a given precision) we test the trajectory modeling capacity of the RNN. A novel trajectory (not used for learning) has been generated (Fig. 7B, open circles curve). The first three points of the trajectory have been used to estimate the initial conditions, i.e. the vector $\xi(0)$ in (14). Then this vector has been submitted to the RNN as external activation to simulate trajectories using the coupling matrices obtained at 5% and 0.5% precision (open squares and triangles in Fig. 7B, respectively). With 5% error the trajectory simulated by the network significantly diverges from the real one. However, with improved learning (10 additional training cycles) the simulated trajectory reproduces the real one with a high precision.

3.3 Learning and retrieval of CIRs

Let us describe the RNN used to learn and later retrieve CIRs. As mentioned above each CIR can be considered as a static 2D pattern, $\{r^*_{ij}\}^m_{i,j=1}$, which can be (arbitrarily) ordered into a 1D vector of length m^2.

Let us assume that p such vectors or different CIRs: $\{a_1, a_2, \ldots, a_p\} \subset \mathbb{R}^{m^2}$ $(p \leq m^2)$ compose a learning set for the RNN consisting of m^2 units (Fig. 6). At each learning step k the network is exposed to one of the vectors and the learning follows the rule for static cases (K′uhn et al., 2007; Makarov et al., 2008):

$$W(k+1) = W(k)\left(I - \varepsilon\xi(k)\xi^T(k)\right) + \varepsilon\xi(k)\xi^T(k) \tag{15}$$

where $\varepsilon > 0$ is the learning rate and $\xi(k)$ is the training external activation applied to the network (i.e. one of the vectors $a_1, \ldots, a_p$ for each k). We note that at each step the coupling matrix is updated by a single vector independently on the other elements in the training sequence.

To be successfully learned, all training vectors should appear sufficiently frequently in the learning sequence and be linearly independent[5], i.e. $\langle a_i, a_j \rangle \neq 0 \ \forall i \neq j$. The former means that the occurrence frequency of the i-th vector

$$f_i = \lim_{k\to\infty} \frac{k_i}{k}$$

is greater then zero (k_i is the number of the vector's occurrences up to time k).

3.3.1 Convergence of the network training procedure

It has been shown (Makarov et al., 2008) that the learning of static situations (i.e. of CIRs) can be always achieved by using a small enough learning rate satisfying to:

$$0 < \varepsilon < \min\left\{\frac{2}{\|a_1\|^2}, \frac{2}{\|a_2\|^2}, \ldots, \frac{2}{\|a_p\|^2}\right\} \tag{16}$$

The learning result (in terms of W_∞) does not depend on the sequence of the presentation of the training vectors $a_1, \ldots, a_p$ to the network. The latter, for instance, means that training by a periodic sequence of two vectors (e.g., $\xi(t) = a_1, a_2, a_1, a_2, a_1, \ldots$) gives the same matrix W_∞ as the training by a random sequence of these vectors (e.g., $\xi(k) = a_1, a_1, a_2, a_1, a_1, a_1, a_2, a_2, a_1, \ldots$), even if the probability to find vector a_1 is different from the

[5] In the case of linearly dependent vectors, the learning goes on a maximal linearly independent subset of the training matrix (Makarov et al., 2008).

probability to find vector a_2. For practical implementation, we note that the learning time scales as

$$T_{\text{training}} \propto \frac{1}{\min\left(f_i \ln \frac{1}{1-\varepsilon\|a_i\|^2}\right)}$$

Thus an excessively small learning rate and/or small occurrence frequency of one of the training vectors deteriorates the learning performance. This particularly means that the network can learn equally well, say two vectors a_1 and a_2, even if the occurrence frequency of one of them is much smaller then that of the other (e.g., $f_1 \ll f_2$), however the training time in this case will be proportionally longer, i.e. $T_{\text{training}} \propto 1/f_1$.
The learning process (15) converges to the coupling matrix (Makarov et al., 2008):

$$W_\infty = \sum_{i=1}^{p} \frac{c_i c_i^T}{\|c_i\|^2} \tag{17}$$

where the vectors

$$c_1 = a_1, \quad c_i = a_i - \sum_{j=1}^{i-1} \frac{\langle a_i, c_j \rangle}{\| c_j \|^2} c_j \quad \text{for } 2 \le i \le p \tag{18}$$

form an orthogonal set due to Gram-Schmidt orthogonalization procedure (Strang, 2003). Thus the RNN composed of n neurons can learn up to n different CIRs described by nD vectors. In other words the learning efficiency approaches the striking value of one CIR per one neuron.

3.3.2 Retrieval of learned patterns

Let us assume that the network previously learned a set of p CIRs $\{a_1, a_2, \ldots a_p\}$. Thus the inter-neuronal couplings are given by (17). Then the retrieval of one of the learned CIRs is achieved by presenting to the RNN (and maintaining during the retrieval process) a small piece (cue) of this CIR.
Without loss of generality we can assume that a fraction of the pattern shown to the RNN for the retrieval corresponds to the first l elements of the pattern a_1 ($1 \le l < n$). Thus the network activation is given by[6]

$$\xi_{1,\ldots,l}(k) = a_{1;1,\ldots,l} \qquad \xi_{l+1,\ldots,n}(k) = 0, \qquad k \ge 0$$

Consequently the first l neurons in the RNN have no dynamics:

$$x_{1,\ldots,l}(k) = a_{1;1,\ldots,l}, \qquad k \ge 0$$

while the others follow the linear map:

$$y(k+1) = \hat{W} y(k) + B, \qquad \hat{W} = (w_{ij}^\infty), \ \forall i,j = l+1,\ldots,n, \qquad B = \sum_{j=1}^{l} w_{ij}^\infty a_{1;j} \tag{19}$$

where (w_{ij}^∞) is given by (17) and $y(0) = 0$. One can show that the eigenvalues of W_∞ are:

$$\lambda_{1,\ldots,p} = 1 \qquad \lambda_{p+1,\ldots,n} = 0$$

[6] Here $a_{i;j}$ means the j-th element of the i-th vector.

whereas $\hat{W}$ has a similar set but l of them satisfy to $0 < \lambda < 1$. Thus the map (19) converges to a fixed point. The set of fixed points of the map (19) corresponds to:

$$(I - \hat{W})\bar{y} = B$$

Then by direct substitution one can check that $\bar{y} = a_{1;l+1,\ldots,n}$. In other words the RNN completes the missing part of a_1 and hence retrieves the original stimulus.

3.3.3 Numerical simulations

Figure 8A shows a (64 × 48)-pixels image, which we divided into two parts (left and right) representing static 2D patterns I_1 and I_2, (32 × 48)-elements each. The gray intensity of these patterns has been mapped into the range $[0,1]$ and then they have been reordered into 1D vectors a_1 and a_2 of the length 1536. During learning we present the training stimuli a_1 and a_2 one after the other to the RNN composed of 1536 neurons. Since each element of the training vectors is bounded we can easily select the learning rate using (16). The lower limit ensuring convergence is $\varepsilon = 2/1536 \approx 0.0013$. To achieve faster convergence we set $\varepsilon = 1.8/\max(\|a_1\|^2, \|a_2\|^2) \approx 0.0024$. The limit coupling matrix W_∞ calculated by (17) has been used to evaluate the learning performance (7). Figure 8B shows that in about 10 training cycles the RNN learns the images I_1 and I_2 with the precision $d(10) \approx 1\%$, whereas for 20 training cycles it approaches $d(20) = 4.5 \times 10^{-4}\%$.
Once the training has been performed, the learned coupling matrix $W(20)$ has been fixed and we test the retrieval of learned patterns. For retrieval we use a small fragment of the original images I_1 and I_2 (Fig. 8C, left insets corresponding to iteration 1). One of the fragments has been shown to the RNN while the rest of the external inputs has been set to zero. The network successfully completes both fragments and obtaines the original images I_1 and I_2 with the error (relative mismatch between images) about 10^{-4} in 100 iterations. It is noteworthy that during retrieval at the beginning there appear a mixture of both images and then the correct one "attracts" the network state. For example at iteration 10 during retrieval of I_1 the most recognizable image is I_2 (Fig. 8C, upper line). We also note that besides retrieval of single images the RNN can perform arithmetical operations over them, e.g., by using a linear combination of fragments of two learned images one can obtained the corresponding linear combination in the complete patterns.
In theory retrieval of an image is possible by presenting a single pixel to the RNN, given that the gray intensity for this pixel is different for different images. However, this requires a long retrieval time (number of iterations) and a precise learning (specially in the case of learning of many images). To test how the retrieval time depends on the size of the presented fragment we repeated the image retrieval showing to the network fragments of different size. Figure 8D shows that the retrieval time decreases approximately exponentially with the size of the fragment.

4. Protocognitive behavior

In the previous sections we discussed neural networks essential for building an agent showing protocognitive behavior. Let us now assemble all the networks together and describe how different nontrivial behaviors can be generated, learned, and retrieved on purpose.

4.1 The agent's architecture

Figure 9 shows the general architecture of the agent. The sensory system receives and preprocesses, e.g. visual, information from the environment and extracts geometrical

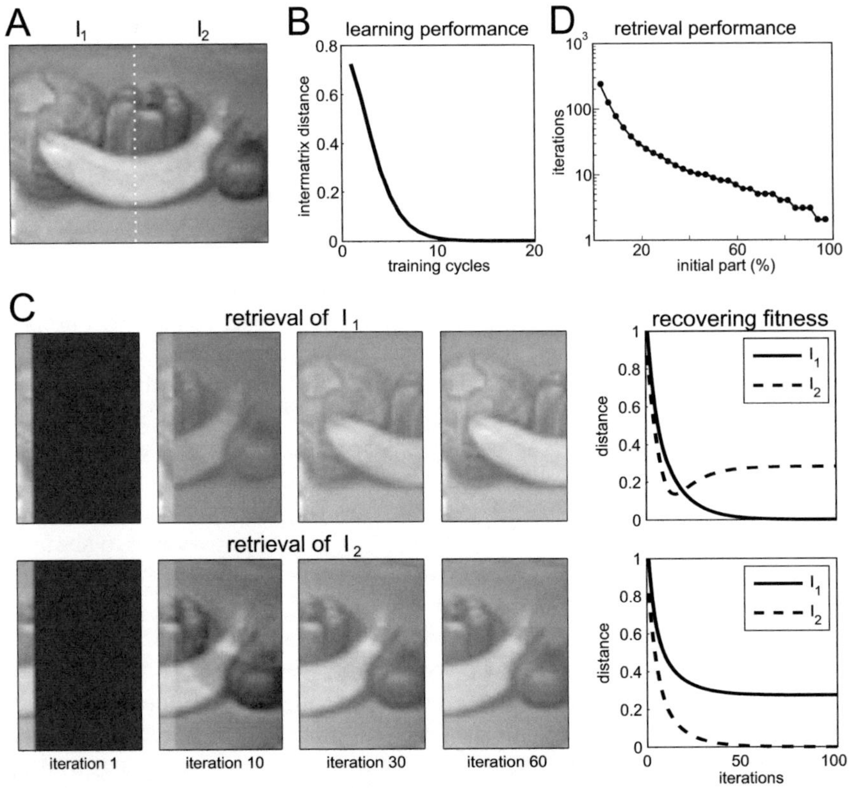

Fig. 8. Learning and retrieval of static 2D patterns by the RNN implementing CIR-memory. A) Original (48 × 64)-image divided into two subimages I_1 and I_2 used for training of the RNN composed of 1536 neurons. B) The learning performance measured by (7). C) Retrieval of the learned images. A fragment of either I_1 (up) or I_2 (bottom) is submitted to the RNN, which completes the image. Right insets show convergence of the image obtained at each iteration of the RNN. D) The retrieval performance. Number of iterations required to obtain the error below 1% versus the size of the fragment shown to the RNN.

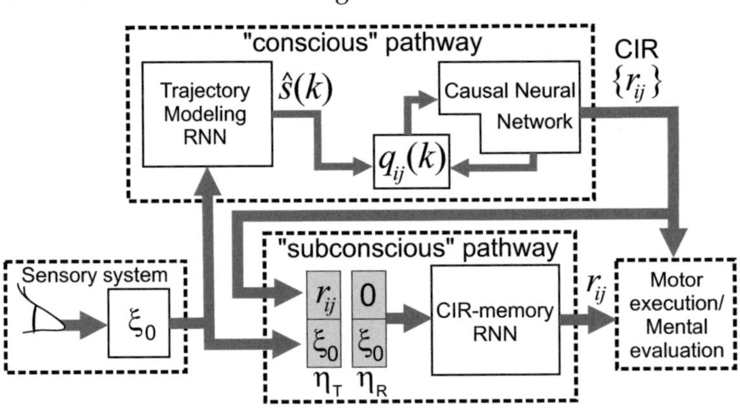

Fig. 9. The agent's architecture and the flow of information.

dimensions, initial positions, velocities, and, if necessary, accelerations of all obstacles/objects in the arena. Besides, the position of a target is defined. The velocity and acceleration are evaluated by (10) using observation of an object in several consecutive time instants. In the simplest case the geometrical dimensions may include length and width of obstacles only. Then it is sufficient to track the geometrical centers of the obstacles, while the rest can be obtained by translation.

The sensory information at $t = 0$, coded by an uD vector $\xi_0 \in \Xi \subset \mathbb{R}^u$, is supplied to: i) Slow "conscious" and ii) Fast "subconscious" pathways (Fig. 9). Both pathways at the outputs produce CIRs corresponding to the observed dynamical situation, i.e. patterns $\{r^*_{ij}\} \in R \subset \mathbb{R}^{m^2}_+$. The difference among them resides in the response-time and precision. The conscious pathway generates accurate CIRs, however it may take too long time, whereas the subconscious pathway can rapidly retrieve a CIR but the corresponding situation must be previously learned. Depending on the agent's experience and available reaction time either of these CIRs can be used for direct path planning and motor execution. Furthermore, the motor execution can be suppressed and the system can actuate as a part of "autonomous thinking", i.e. instead of sensory information some mental situations can be supplied for evaluation.

4.1.1 Conscious pathway

In the conscious pathway the sensory vector ξ_0 is received by the appropriately tuned Trajectory Modeling RNN (described in Sect. 3.2). This RNN generates in the mental time, $\tau = kh$, trajectories of all obstacles $\hat{s}(k)$. In parallel the Causal Neural Network goes through the process of virtual exploration of the environment (described in Sect. 2). The exploration is based on a wave front propagating in the CNN-lattice and delimiting the virtual present in the mental space-time representation of the agent. The outputs of both networks are used to obtain the binary time dependent pattern $\{q_{ij}(\tau)\}$ by coincidence detection of the wavefront and obstacles' trajectories. This pattern defines effective obstacles and further shapes the relaxation (diffusive) dynamics of the CNN, which finally converges to a static 2D pattern $\{r^*_{ij}\}^m_{i,j=1}$ (or m^2D vector), i.e. to a CIR of the observed situation.

The obtained CIR reproduces faithfully the world model of possible collisions in the future and, in theory, is ready to be used for planning different behaviors. However, the whole process of modeling and creation of a CIR may be slow relatively to the time scale of changes in the environment. Thus the agent requires a mechanism of fast "unconscious" decision making. For this purpose the CIR obtained by the conscious pathway is supplied to the subconscious pathway for learning.

4.1.2 Subconscious pathway

The subconscious pathway is based on the RNN implementing CIR-memory (described in Sect. 3.3). The corresponding RNN operates in the functional space with *extended CIR* vectors given by:

$$\eta = (r^*_{ij}, \xi_0)^T, \qquad \eta \in R \times \Xi = \Pi$$

Thus it expands the functional space of CIRs by adding the relevant sensory information dissected by the sensory system from the raw sensory signals (shape, position, initial velocity of obstacles etc.). The RNN consists of $(m^2 + u)$ neurons: m^2 of them are used to code CIRs (patterns $\{r^*_{ij}\}$), while the remaining u neurons are responsible for coding the sensory vector ξ_0. The CIR-memory can receive (asynchronously) two types of input vectors η: i) CIR

produced by the conscious pathway and the corresponding sensory information (η_T in Fig. 9); and ii) Sensory information with CIR part empty (m^2 zeros) (η_R in Fig. 9).
The first type of inputs, given by the complete vector $\eta_T = (r_{ij}^*, \xi_0)^T$, is used for training the subconscious pathway. We remind that the RNN can learn up to $(m^2 + u)$ different patterns (i.e. extended CIRs). Thus the agent exploring different environments can continuously learn CIRs provided by the conscious pathway and associate them with the corresponding sensory information. Then frequently encountered situations will generate a set of extended CIRs $\{\eta_i\} \subset \Pi$ that will be thoroughly learned. This enables a fast subconscious response of the agent to standard stereotypic situations.
The second type of inputs is given by the vector $\eta_R = (0, \xi_0)^T$ whose first m^2 elements are equal to zero. Such input is used for retrieval of the CIR corresponding to the description of the dynamic situations given by ξ_0. If such a situation (or similar enough) is a standard previously learned situation then the RNN can rapidly complete the missing part in the extended CIR vector η:

$$\text{input: } (0, \xi_0) \quad \rightarrow \quad \text{output: } (r_{ij}^*, \xi_0)^T$$

Thus the agent gets a fast access to CIRs of stereotypic dynamic situations without a need of their modeling by the conscious pathway. This provides the agent with a capability of fast generation of precise behaviors for frequently happening situations.

4.2 Simulations

Let us now illustrate how the agent can cope with dynamical situations and build up libraries of extended CIRs for stereotypic situations and hence behaviors. Figure 10A shows an arena with one static and one moving obstacles interfering the agent's path to the target. We model two similar but different dynamic situations: i) slowly moving obstacle and ii) rapidly moving obstacle. The velocities are chosen such that the moving obstacle blocks either left or right free space from the static obstacle in the time window when the agent can pass there. Then the agent should generate an appropriate behavior and decide on which side it will pass by.
At the beginning the CIR-memory of the agent is empty, and hence the agent can rely on the conscious pathway only. Figure 10B shows two CIRs builded by the conscious pathway and corresponding to the situations with slow and fast obstacle's motions. The mayor difference between them is the position in the lattice space of the effective obstacle blocking the agent movements as it was expected. In the case of slow motion the effective obstacle appears on the left, whereas for the fast motion it appears on the right. Then the optimal paths to the target, safely avoiding obstacles including the moving one, are significantly different in both cases. We note that if CIR is not created "online" by the conscious pathway, then the motor execution cannot be enacted. Instead, the CIR created afterwards serves for learning by the subconscious pathway.
Now we model the process of building a library of extended CIRs. The described situations (slow and fast motions of the obstacle) appear one after another, so the agent repeatedly encounters these situations and creates extended CIRs through the conscious pathway and then learns them in the subconscious pathway. We also assume that the reaction time is critical enough, so the agent has to make a decision on the basis of the output of the subconscious pathway. Figure 10C shows how the agent acquires experience and goes through different stages of the development: from "novice" to "expert".
After three training cycles the subconscious pathway is unable to retrieve successfully CIR corresponding to the situation observed in the environment. Instead the agent "sees" itself in a potential minimum in both situations ("novice" column in Fig. 10C), and hence no

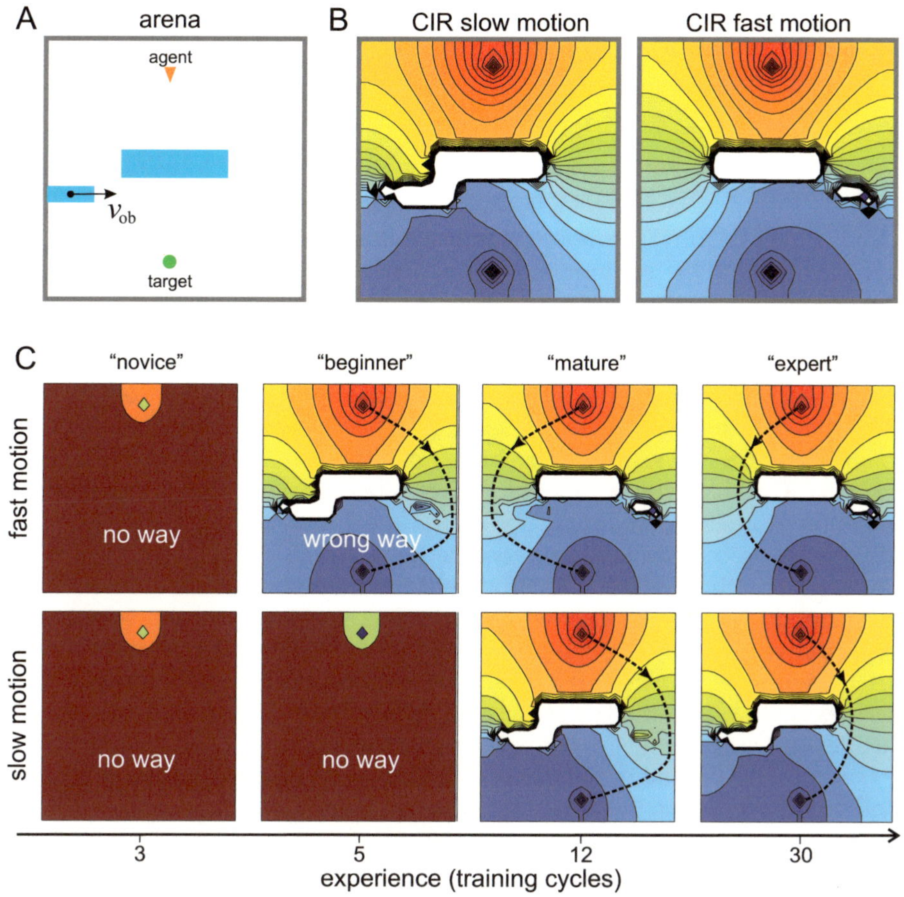

Fig. 10. Simulation of the agent behavior. A) Arena with two obstacles (blue rectangles) one of which moves from left to right with the velocity v_{ob}. B) CIRs obtained by the "conscious" pathway for two different velocities of the moving obstacles: slow (left) and fast (right). C) The process of building CIR-library. The agent generates behaviors based on the output of the subconscious pathway. Dashed curves show optimal trajectories.

trajectory to the target can be traced and the agent cannot reach the target. Getting few more training cycles the subconscious pathway provides a first solution for the case of fast moving obstacle ("beginner" column in Fig. 10C). The obtained CIR allows path-planning, however the agent confuses the CIR corresponding to the slow motion case with the CIR for the fast motion. Consequently the path traced to the target is wrong (unjustifiably risky) for the given situation. It takes about 12 training cycles for the agent to learn correct associations between situations observed in the environment and their CIRs. The agent can now select correct behaviors and pass the obstacles from the left or from the right in accordance with the situation observed in the environment ("mature" column in Fig. 10C). Nevertheless, the provided paths are suboptimal (in length), i.e. they go far away from the identified positions of the effective obstacles. After 30 training cycles the memory is consolidated and the CIRs retrieved from the subconscious pathway are identical to the CIRs obtained by the conscious pathways (compare "expert" column in Fig. 10C and Fig. 10B). Thus in 30 training cycles the agent has successfully built a CIR-library consisting of two similar but different extended CIRs corresponding to two situations that can be encountered in the environment. Now the agent is ready for fast generation of nontrivial precise behaviors relying on the subconscious pathway.

5. Discussion

The main advantage of animate mobile creatures with respect to, e.g., plants is the possibility to actively interact with the environment, which postulates time as a vital dimension. The active interaction with the environment is manifested in a nonrandom purposeful movement, which is a prerequisite of cognition. The agent best dealing with this "extra" dimension receives an evolutionary advantage. The simplest pre-cognitive form of the behavior, adopted by lower organisms, relies on the direct reaction (automatic reflexes) to the sensory stimuli. Although such reactions may be extremely fast, efficient in specific conditions, and even sometimes compound and complex, higher organisms developed significantly different cognitive skills. Thus it has been argued that the global brain function is geared towards the implementation of intelligent motricity [for review see (Llinas & Roy, 2009)].
In this chapter we restricted ourself by considering the problem of generation of behaviors by a mobile agent in time-evolving environments as a paradigm of real situations faced by living beings (Fig. 1). We have shown that a solution of this problem may be described as a protocognitive process composing first floors of the Cognitive Pyramid. It includes (at least) the following four "bricks" (Fig. 9): i) sensory system; ii) "conscious" pathway; iii) "subconscious" pathway; and iv) motor system. Let us briefly summarize their main features and principles of operation.
i) *Sensory system*. The amount of information contained in the environment in principle may tend to infinity, in part due to the presence of the time dimension. In general, the current state of the environment is an element of a functional space $x \in X \times (-\infty, 0]$, where X describes the spatial structure of the environment. Thus at the first step the sensory system should brake this continuum and extract the information required by the agent for achieving a goal (i.e. construction of a behavior). In the simplest case (e.g., for path-planning) the state of the environment can be reduced to a finite-dimensional vector $\xi_0 \in \Xi \subset \mathbb{R}^u$ coding the shapes of the objects, their initial positions and velocities. Thus the sensory system drastically reduces the dimension of the available information and represents it in the form of a static pattern, $g_{t_0} : X \times (-\infty, 0] \to \Xi$, conveyed to the conscious and subconscious pathways.
ii) *Conscious pathway*. On the next step the spatially coded information, ξ_0, provided by the sensory system is used for prediction of virtual futures with the aim of anticipation of, e.g., collisions with obstacles. In general, the world model should deal with three conceptually different objects: a) the external inanimate or unintelligent objects; b) the agent itself; and c) other animate agents either cooperating or competing for resources (for the sake of simplicity we excluded such case). We have shown that a specially trained recurrent neural network can successfully predict trajectories of inanimate objects thus solving the item (a). The (imaginary) behavior of the agent is essentially not unique and can be and must be adapted to the external circumstances. This, in theory, may increase dramatically the dimension of the state variable describing the virtual futures. Thus the central issue in brain functions is the optimization of the mapping of the external environment and, more importantly, of the agent itself (self-awareness) into an internal functional space followed by a *join* IR. Some authors propose that the internal space should be isomorphic to the external world. However, this would overload the brain with unnecessary information. To optimize the information

processing we proposed to relax the isomorphic condition to a surjection mapping, i.e. to $f : \Xi \to R \subset \mathbb{R}^{m^2}$ such that for every $r \in R$ in the codomain (internal space) there is a $\xi_0 \in \Xi$ in the domain (sensory image) such that $f(\xi_0) = r$. Although conceptually simple such mapping is not trivial to be implemented in a neural network. The network should go through two concurrent processes: a) divergence of information due to generation of virtual futures and b) convergence or compaction of virtual futures into a static structure or multi-dimensional vector r. Our approach is based on the concept of Compact Internal Representations of time-evolving environments (Villacorta-Atienza et al., 2010). We have been able to build a 2D neural network (Causal Neural Network) that exploits the principle of causality, which enables reduction of the time-dependent structure of real situations to compact static patterns. Due to compactness the resulting patterns (i.e. elements of R) are suitable to be learned, stored and recovered on request of higher cognitive levels.
iii) *Subconscious pathway*. Another problem to be resorted is the time of response. Behaviors made on the basis of internal representations may be very flexible and comprehensive. However, the agent may lose considerably to the reaction of reflex-like precognitive agents. Thus a learning process, which transforms behaviors into subconscious reflex-like states, is essential for the intelligent motricity. To implement subconscious behaviors we used a recurrent neural network that is able to learn and retrieve static patterns. We have introduced the extended CIR space $\Pi = R \times \Xi$, which includes both Compact Internal Representations (generated by the "conscious" pathway) and the corresponding state vectors provided by the sensory system. We have shown that the agent can learn extended CIRs, which form a plexus of attractors in the phase space of the RNN. Then any previously learned extended CIR $\eta \in \Pi$ can be rapidly retrieved by presenting to the subconscious pathway the sensory part only, i.e. showing $\xi_0 \in \Xi$ receive $r \in R$. This enables fast reflex-like retrieval of stereotypic CIRs from a "library" $\{r_k\} \subset R$ corresponding to situation frequently observed in the environment.
iv) *Motor system*. The motor execution of behaviors is based on the tracing paths in CIRs using given by higher cognitive levels criteria $h : R \to S$, where S is a space of trajectories. For example the agent can optimize the length of the path or its safety (distance to obstacles). This criteria can also include additional constraints like 'pass through a particular point', etc.
Thus we suggest that cognition appears as an effective method of processing, storing and retrieval of time-dependent sensory information, based on compact internal representations, with the aim of construction of behaviors and active interaction with the environment: $g_{t_0} \circ f \circ h : X \times (-\infty, 0] \to S$.

6. Acknowledgments

This study has been supported by the Spanish Ministry of Science and Innovation (MICINN) under the grants: FIS2007-65173 and FIS2010-20054, and a Juan de la Cierva fellowship awarded to J.A.V-A.

7. References

Baars, B.J. & Gage, N.M. (2010). *Cognition, Brain, and Consciousness: Introduction to Cognitive Neuroscience*. Academic Press (2nd edit.)

Bear, M.F.; Conners, B.W. & Paradiso, M.A. (2007). *Neuroscience: exploring the brain*. Williams & Wilkins. 3rd Ed.

Cruse, H. (2003). The evolution of cognition - a hypothesis. *Cognitive Science*, Vol. 27, 135-155

Godfrey-Smith, P. (2001). Environmental Complexity and the Evolution of Cognition. In *The evolution of intelligence* (Sternberg R. and Kaufman J. eds.) Lawrence Erlbaum Associates

Hesslow, G. (2002). Conscious thought as simulation of behaviour and perception. *Trends in Cognitive Sciences,* Vol. 6, 242-247

Kandel, E.R.; Schwartz, J.H. & Jessell, T.M. (2000). *Principles of neural science.* New York: McGraw-Hill, 4th ed.

Keymeulen, D. & Decuyper, J. (1994). The fluid dynamics applied to mobile robot motion: the stream field method. *Proceedings IEEE Int Conf on Robotics and Automation,* 378-385

K′uhn, S.; Beyn W.J. & Cruse, H. (2007). Modelling memory functions with recurrent neural networks consisting of input compensation units: I. Static situations. *Biological Cybernetics,* Vol. 96, 455-470

Llinas, R.R. & Roy, S. (2009). The 'prediction imperative' as the basis for self-awareness. *Philosophical Transactions of the Royal Society B,* Vol. 364, 1301-1307

Louste, C. & Liegeois, A. (2000). Near optimal robust path planning for mobile robots: the viscous fluid method with friction. *Journal of Intell and Robotic Systems,* Vol. 27, 99-112

Makarov, V.A.; Song, Y.; Velarde, M.G.; H′ubner, D. & Cruse, H. (2008). Elements for a general memory structure: properties of recurrent neural networks used to form situation models. *Biological Cybernetics,* Vol. 98, 371-395

McIntyre, J.; Zago, M.; Berthoz, A. & Lacquaniti, F. (2001). Does the brain model Newton's laws? *Nature Neurosci,* Vol. 4, 693-694

Nekorkin, V.I. & Makarov, V.A. (1995). Spatial chaos in a chain of coupled bistable oscillators. *Physical Review Letters,* Vol. 74, 4819-4822

Nekorkin, V.I.; Makarov, V.A.; Kazantsev, V.B. & Velarde, M.G. (1997). Spatial disorder and pattern formation in lattices of coupled elements. *Physica D,* Vol. 100, 330-342

Newell, A. (1994). *Unified theories of cognition.* Harvard University Press.

Savelli, F.; Yoganarasimha, D. & Knierim, J.J. (2008). Influence of boundary removal on the spatial representations of the medial entorhinal cortex. *Hippocampus,* Vol. 18(12), 1270-1282

Schmidt, G.K. & Azarm, K. (1992). Mobile robot navigation in a dynamic world using an unsteady diffusion equation strategy. *Proceedings IEEE/RSJ Int Conf Intelligent Robots and Systems,* 642-647

Sepulchre, J.A. & MacKay, R.S. (1997). Localized oscillations in conservative or dissipative networks of weakly coupled autonomous oscillators. *Nonlinearity,* Vol. 10, 679-713

Strang, G. (2003). *Introduction to Linear Algebra.* Wellesley-Cambridge Press.

Villacorta-Atienza, J.A.; Velarde, M.G. & Makarov, V.A. (2010). Compact internal representation of dynamic situations: Neural network implementing the causality principle. *Biological Cybernetics,* Vol. 103, 285-297

Wasserman, E.A. & Zentall, T.R. (2009). *Comparative Cognition: Experimental Explorations of Animal Intelligence.* Oxford University Press US.

Wray, R.; Lebiere, C.; Weinstein, P.; Jha, K.; Springer, J.; Belding T.; Best, B. & Parunak V. (2007). Towards a Complete, Multi-level Cognitive Architecture. In *Proc of the International Conference for Cognitive Modeling,* Ann Arbor, MI, July 27-29.